Reverend G's Words of Encouragement

My Journey and Life's Lessons Along the Way
"I Could Blame Others, but I Won't"

Reverend Jeffery E. Gaines Sr.

iUniverse books may be ordered through booksellers or by contacting:

iUniverse
1663 Liberty Drive
Bloomington, IN 47403
www.iuniverse.com
844-349-9409

Because of the dynamic nature of the Internet, any web addresses or links contained in this book may have changed since publication and may no longer be valid. The views expressed in this work are solely those of the author and do not necessarily reflect the views of the publisher, and the publisher hereby disclaims any responsibility for them.

Any people depicted in stock imagery provided by Getty Images are models, and such images are being used for illustrative purposes only. Certain stock imagery © Getty Images.

Unless otherwise indicated, all scripture quotations are from The Holy Bible, English Standard Version® (ESV®). Copyright ©2001 by Crossway Bibles, a division of Good News Publishers. Used by permission. All rights reserved.

ISBN: 978-1-6632-3767-5 (sc)
ISBN: 978-1-6632-3656-2 (e)

Library of Congress Control Number: 2022905301

Print information available on the last page.

iUniverse rev. date: 03/25/2022

Table of Contents

Dedication

This book is dedicated to my wife, Brenda "BG", who has stood by my side through the test of time. BG is my ride or die partner for life. To my son Jeffery Jr., his wife Ryann, my daughter Candice and her husband Anthony, and my amazing grandkids Matthew, Brooklynn, Logyn, and Myles, and all future grandkids, Papa loves all of you.

Acknowledgements

There are so many people that I have to say thank you to that I cannot place all their names here, so please know that if your name is not listed, it is only a reflection of the space available on the page and not the space available in my heart of thanks. That being said, my first thanks goes out to my greatest hero, Lou Jean Gaines, my mom. Although she is resting safely in heaven, without her love and her kind words, I would not have become the man I am today. I also want to acknowledge Annie Nelson, the sweetest mother-in-law in the galaxy, who is also resting in heaven, for being my second mom, correcting me when I needed it and loving me when I did not deserve it. To my siblings (Wilbert, Alberta, Bernadette, Teresa, Tammy, and Benjamin) for being by my side and sticking with me through thick and thin. To Todd and Kathy, my Marine friends, who hold to the creed of iron sharpens iron. As a preacher you are limited in who you can really be down to earth with and talk to about any or all things. I am fortunate to have had at least two ministers in my life: Elder Aaron Matlock, who is resting in the gentle arms of Jesus, and Reverend Dennis Drake. Elder Matlock, I miss you man; you were the man of wisdom and laughter, and not to mention a man of style. To Reverend Drake, the guy I call anytime and vent or bounce a sermon off before preaching it, thank you, brother. Of course, I want to thank my longest running man and friend of over fifty-five years, Malcolm aka "Tick." This dude was my own personal bodyguard in school and hanging out at the club, love you man. Of course, to the best vacation friends in the whole wide world, Hebert and Roycea. It was an honor and privilege to serve in the military and I served with some great commanders, but my most lasting commander is CPT Oakley. Thank you, sir, for taking care of the troops. Lastly, to all of my church families over the years, thank you for your prayers and words of encouragement. I could not overcome without your support and correction.

Introduction

Everyone has a story to tell, and my story is not that much different than yours. But for those who have endured and overcome many struggles in this life, my story is to encourage you further in life, to keep on living. That being said, my story begins as a native Floridian who grew up poor, on welfare, a high school dropout and without a father, who abandoned me at an incredibly early age in my life. But what I have learned in this life is that sometimes we are born in a disadvantaged situation, either being poor or dependent upon federal assistance for food and clothing. Combine that with a broken family structure, this lent itself to a life of struggles and setbacks. God knows I had a lot of them. And for years, if not decades, I blamed others for how I felt and how my life was turning out. Granted even to this day these individuals earned the banner of shameful treatment toward Jeffery Gaines, but blame was not going to change the trajectory of my life. I had a decision to make: I could either decide to remain in the state of blaming others or I could get off my backside and do something about it. I decided to go with the latter, and I hope that you will come to the same decision after hearing my story.

Please do not get me wrong–while I chose the latter, it was not an overnight decision. No, my friend, I endured some unspeakable atrocities inflicted upon me as a kid, so it took me some time to move forward in confidence and defiance. This meant I was involved in drugs, alcohol, and misdemeanor criminal activities, but for the record, no felonies. That being said, my life had its good moments from childhood to parenthood, and so many amazing dreams have come true for me. I hope that after reading my book you will walk away with a sense that this ordinary guy went through extraordinary challenges in life—some created by others and some of his own making, but with God's grace, he is not blaming others but deciding to pursue life's dreams. Please go and do likewise.

My Early Life Journey

Growing up in Rural Central Florida

To give you a well-rounded view of my background, I will start with my upbringing and how I saw life unfold around me in so many ways that I cannot count them all.

First, the earliest memories I can recall start when I was about two years old living in a place called Dunnellon, Florida; and yes, before you Google it, Dunnellon still exists, and by all accounts is flourishing and growing. While we did not live in the actual city limits of Dunnellon, we were on the outskirts of the town in a place referred to as the Sawmill Quarters, which is next to a place called Chatmire, and likewise, it is still there today but not as it looked and felt so many years ago. I did not know at the time that it was called Sawmill Quarters because we were located right next to a sawmill factory that trimmed trees and produced building lumber. Our little wooden frame shotgun home was located right next to the railroad tracks, and we would always hear the train pass by as it carried its cargo to locations across Florida. In our home there was no electricity, no centralized heating or air conditioning. Neither was there any running water because we did not have plumbing. Thus, there was the outhouse a few feet away in the backyard. However, living there was such a fun time in my life. There were only about eight to ten homes in this area. This meant a small circle of friends. I could simply walk over to their front porch and hang out. We could just be kids on a dirt road relaxing and having fun.

To me these were fond memories because my father worked at the sawmill on one of those big saws that produced planks of lumber. He would often come home smelling like sawdust as he consumed lunch that Mom prepared for him. Speaking of my mother, I remember her as a stay-at-home mom because at that time, I was the youngest of four children. She spent all of her time taking care of us and cleaning that little ole wooden shack next to the railroad tracks. Yes, we were poor, but for me it just seems like a natural state of life. As I see it, I was a happy child and thought we had a great life. However, I had no idea that my mom and dad were having marital problems. Though they never told me, nor did I ever learn what their problems were, they decided to part ways. This parting of ways changed my life and the outcomes of my life even until this very day.

> **Reverend G's Lesson for You:** *You can blame the circumstances of your early life, or you can use those circumstances to propel you beyond other people's expectations and more importantly beyond your own expectations of yourself.*

After My Parents' Divorce, Life Becomes Hellish at Best

To all those who say Hell does not exist, I say, you do not know what in the hell you are talking about. Now let me tell you about Hell. To my memory, I believe my parents separated when I was around the tender age of five. As a result of that event, my life literally became a living hell, and hell might be putting it lightly. To start with, my father never had a conversation with me about the divorce. He just packed up one day and walked away, leaving us to fend for ourselves. Needless to say, when you are a stay-at-home mom and all of sudden the person who was providing income just leaves the family, your life becomes filled with uncertainty and is chaotic at best. My life was no different.

The day came when Mom and Dad separated, and we had to leave our wooden shack by the railroad track. While I was young, I dreaded the idea of leaving the place in which I had enjoyed hanging out with my friends. I had no idea where we were moving to and who we were moving in with. It was then that I found myself in this even more remote place on the side of the road called Romeo, Florida. Trust me, the name Romeo may conjure up romance, but there was nothing romantic about the little country roadside stop. Romeo, while not much to see, was full of people who just worked hard and tried to enjoy their weekend off. I mean, it was another small community and is even smaller today. If I had to put a number on those who lived in close proximity to our home, I would say fifty at best. There were no streetlights; when nightfall came it was completely dark outside which meant we had to be inside or experience the wrath of breaking curfew. But on the flip side there were things I really liked about Romeo, like the fishing ponds, going hunting right out the back door, and climbing the large trees in my neighbors' yard. To a certain degree, Romeo felt better

than the Sawmill Quarters because of the country feel of fresh air and gardens right outside in front. Plus, we no longer lived right next to railroad tracks which meant days and nights were much more peaceful, or so I thought.

Though the home that we moved into was better than the house we left, it still lacked running water, and the outhouse was located further into the woods than one can imagine. This made for some scary trips to use the bathroom at night. My life became a living nightmare because of the man my mother came to love and cherish. That man was my stepfather, and trust me, I use the term stepfather simply for the purpose of connecting with readers of this book. He literally hated my guts and probably told me this on a daily basis. His treatment of the children in his care was horrendous. But by far, the children that were not his biologically, received the worst possible care one could imagine. He constantly told me how worthless I was and how I would never amount to anything. And yes, I grew up thinking I was worthless, but more on that later. I want to describe a typical weekend trying to survive my stepfather.

It always started on Fridays because that was payday for my stepfather and meant that he could buy all the liquor he wanted and become drunk beyond comprehension. He was always mean, but when he became drunk, he took on a meanness that would make the devil seem like your best friend, and this is not an exaggeration. He cursed us out for no reason, and one thing he loved doing was beating us with whatever he could get his hands on. Mind you I said beating, not spanking. There was a time when we would get beat with a water hose or an electrical extension cord. There were times when beating was not enough and he would exact torture and torment. For example, I distinctly remember one day I was hungry, so I decided to take a spoon full of peanut butter from one of those large gallon size cans of peanut butter provided to us by Florida's welfare department. Well, my stepfather found out about it and force-fed me the entire can of peanut butter. I do not recall if I was able to eat the entire can, but I do remember being fearful not to try because that would mean an instant belt or stick to my bare back side. This went on throughout my youth, from age five to seventeen.

As each year went by, he became more evil and wicked and creative in new ways to punish the stepchildren; mind you he did not treat his biological children that much better. There is a claim that it does not get cold in Florida; this is an absolute false assumption because it does get extremely cold during some winters. I say this to lead into one of the most dangerous things my stepfather did to me. There was one occasion during the middle of winter that he kicked me and my older brother out of the house and made us sleep in an animal shed with no heating or lighting. My brother and I had to literally hug each other for warmth to keep from

freezing to death. One night the temperature dropped so much that my brother and I had to build a fire with newspaper in an old auto hubcap to try and keep warm. We cried all night long from the pain of the cold chilling our bones. Why didn't we rebel? Of course, when you live with terror, you tend to obey your captor because of that fear. However, guess who found out about it and instructed us never to do it again? If it had not been for my wife's grandfather forcing him to allow us back into the house, I earnestly believe my brother and I would have gotten frostbite, or worse, died in that animal shed. I could go on and on about how he shot at us, threatened to cut my throat, and refused to let a terrified young boy sleep with the light on. But I believe you get the point as to how awful life was for me with my stepfather.

One point I have not stated is the love between the step siblings. I do not have any recollection of us ever referring to ourselves as step siblings. We were all in the same boat and I think we survived because we kept each other encouraged and out of harm's way as much as possible. Even as I grew older, my stepfather never really recognized me as a human being. All he could see was a little dark-skinned boy with nappy hair. For some bizarre reason he was big on skin complexion, and he always reminded me of how much less of a person I was because of the dark complexion of my skin. However, on the flip side he took immense joy in the fact that children he had conceived with my mother were of lighter complexion. Mind you they were still treated harshly but were not subject to the dark skin debasement and humiliation that I experienced up until the day I left home for good. As I stated earlier, I was around five years old when my stepfather entered my life, so it was easy for him to instill fear into my heart and hard for me to overcome that fear, no matter how much I wanted to. I just could not do it of my own strength and courage. However, as I began to enter my teen years, I quickly realized that I was in a life-or-death situation. In other words, I was going to kill him, or he was going to kill me. It was at this time I decided I had to do something, or my life would forever be in jeopardy.

> **Reverend G's Lesson for You:** *I could blame my father for leaving me, and I do. I could blame my stepfather for my lack of self-esteem, and he is absolutely responsible for it. However, these men have lived their lives and cannot do anything to change my life. So rather than letting their actions dictate my future, I am deciding to use their actions to propel me to new levels of success in life. Can you do the same thing? I hope so.*

School Days – I Am Glad That Is Behind Me

Early School Years

Let me say for the record that I liked school, but it is not for the reason you think. School for me was a chance to get away from my stepfather. Attending school only meant a lesser hell for a few hours of the day, and I grabbed even that small respite. See, when you are poor, there is no mercy from other students, and in some cases the teachers. In short, I was horrible at academics, but I would like to think that was because of my home life. The only subject I was good at was lunch. My grades were dismal from elementary to high school. In fact, in elementary school I was placed in special education classes because I could not read nor write, and even to this date, I struggle in these areas. Placing me in special education classes only added to the harassment I was receiving from other students, which in my mind made me suck even more at school. Of course, being poor and wearing hand-me-down clothing made me a target for teachers as well. Case in point. As a child I had grown a large afro. The problem was I could not afford to go to the barber shop on a regular basis which meant there were days I went to school with unkempt hair. Well, one day my elementary school teacher (whose name will remain unmentioned) decided she was going to comb my hair. Mind you she did not pull me aside privately. No, she decided to march me up front so the entire class could observe this public torture of a young poor black child. She sat me down, pulled out a comb, and commenced to try to comb my hair with all the strength she could muster. If you have never grown an afro, you may not be able to relate to the pain that shoots through your scalp as someone tries to pull all the kinks out your nappy mate. I sat there no longer able to hold back the tears and anguish while all my classmates laughed and teased me for years to come about that incident. Personally, I do not think I ever recovered from that shame until I reached my early thirties.

Somehow by the grace of God I managed to get through elementary school and found myself doing okay in middle school. However, that is where things went from bad to worse as I started high school. When I entered Dunnellon High School, I was constantly bullied verbally and physically. I was always timid and

never really fought back. Simply put, I chose to endure it, which looking back was the wrong approach. The only thing that reduced my bully events was my best friend. He was my bodyguard, and he was built for the struggle that I could not overcome. Nothing but muscles and a good heart. He and I became like Batman and Robin, and when you picked on Jeff, Batman would swoop in and deliver swift and intense justice. So, trust me, when he said he was sick and could not go to school, I was sick and could not go to school because I knew what would happen if my perpetrators knew he was not around. Our friendship grew from elementary even until today—a friendship of over fifty years in the making.

Gaining an Early, Invaluable Work Ethic

Working on Other People's Farms

Some people say working on the farm is challenging work. Personally, I must take exception and say working on other people's farms is probably the hardest, most unrewarding work I have ever done. Oh, please do not get me wrong. Farming is a wonderful thing if you are the beneficiary of all the arduous work. However, if you are a child, it is akin to forced labor. I landed my first job at the tender age of nine with the neighbor who took me to work with him on farms in the Central Florida region. I have to admit it was fun during that period because he took the time to explain everything we were doing. He would encourage me, and that was a far different treatment than what my stepfather was doing, so I loved working on the farm at the age of nine. However, as a teenager it was no longer fun for me. I had to do it because it was necessary, and all my money went toward the household budget. We were so poor it was expected that any additional money went straight to Mom's budget for food and supplies, which was fine by me because Mom would also slide me some cash under the table when my stepfather was not looking. However, this meant my stepfather made me go to work for people who did not always treat me fairly nor give me fair pay for a grueling day's work on the farm. I worked the fields bailing hay, loading watermelons, lifting pulp wood, and slopping hogs, and I hated every minute of it. The only good part about working on the farms was I could spend time with my friends who were also always working the fields. The strange thing about me working the fields was I would often hear adults complimenting me on how good a job I was doing and how they would trust me with higher responsibilities. I thought nothing of it at the time, but my ability to accomplish downright grueling work turned out to be a game-changer in my military career. However, back to the farm.

My life had become so connected to working the farms that before long we had to labor on farms prior to school attendance each morning. I can remember many mornings the hay hauling truck pulling up to take us to work before the sun rose, only to drop us off at the local gas station so we could wash off in the bathroom before going to school. Can you imagine what it is like to walk around school smelling like animals and how students treated you? I hope not.

> **Reverend G's Lesson for You:** *Challenging work is good for the character and none of us should shun it. However, you can work hard for others, or you can work hard for yourself. Who do you prefer to be your boss?*

By far, high school was the worst period in my academic journey. I cannot even begin to tell you how awful my report cards were, and my behavior suffered. I failed at so many grades I cannot remember them all. My behavior was abhorrent because I only came to school to get away from my stepfather, so learning was never my objective. It was just a temporary escape. It may be hard to imagine but there was a time when the principal would spank me on the butt with a paddling board. I found myself in the principal's office often, and yes, I was paddled by a white man that did not understand a young black person from a broken family. If there ever was a time I should have thrown a punch, this would have been it, but I did not. I endured as always and suffered in silence.

During my high school years, I dreaded going to the bathroom because I was often cornered and bullied. While I loved physical education class, the nightmare continued when I had to go to the locker room and endure the harassment of not having the proper clothing for physical exercise. By the way, I sucked at sports and even today am not good at them. I hated the idea of being on the softball field and dreaded the possibility that the ball could be hit in my direction. But as luck or bad luck would have it, I often found myself out in center field and the ball was hit high in the air. I placed my glove in the proper place anticipating that I would be the hero for catching it. Then it happened. The ball barely missed the top of my glove and hit me right between the eyes. Mind you it was painful but not as painful as the ridicule that followed for years to come. To this date I hate playing softball. However, I did have a sliver of good news. I loved to run because I was always running from the bullies in school. So, I do remember doing well in some of the running events. At the time I did not know it would be a Godsend for me later in life.

I guess the straw that broke the proverbial camel's back is when I found out I had failed in high school, and they were going to hold me back from going to the next grade. I thought my life was over because I knew it would be a walking hell for me to hear from all of my classmates who had moved on. It was only by the grace of God that my mom decided to send me to another school because I had enough credits not to be held back. This marked a new chapter in life and a whole new attitude toward learning. For it was then that I realized I was not stupid or dumb but just in a bad living environment. In the new school no one knew about all the stuff I had suffered, and I never experienced any bullying at the new school (thank you Williston High School). By all accounts I was doing much better, and my grades were on the uptick.

> **Reverend G's Lesson for You:** *I could blame my stepfather, and heck yes, I still do blame him for the torment. However, I can only blame myself if I choose to allow his actions to hold me back from the good things in life.*

Failing Grades and Dropping out of High School

While my transition to a new school had placed me on a better academic path, it did not change the stepfather situation which ultimately impacted my ability to focus on school, resulting in poor grades. I knew I was not going to finish high school even though I had made it to the eleventh grade. I could not see myself surviving that long to graduate. I needed to do something to change my environment, but I had no idea what that would be. I tried running away from home but became scared after I had walked beyond the glow of the streetlights.

Joining the Military Changed the Trajectory of My Life

As I mentioned earlier, I knew my life was in danger at home, and I had to do something to change the environment. Either my stepfather had to leave, or I had to leave. Since I knew there was zero chance of him going anywhere, I realized I had to find a way out from under his toxic impact in my life. This meant I had to drop out of high school and leave Romeo if I were ever going to live a normal life.

Suddenly a remarkably familiar face showed up back in Romeo. At that time, I had no inkling that I would find my inspiration and escape vehicle for a new life in the military. That familiar face was a childhood friend by the name of Brenda Nelson. Brenda was the cute little six-year-old girl, and when I was five years old, I used to admire her from afar because I was too afraid to approach her. However, one day I did approach her, and Brenda and I became friends; in fact, we became really good friends. Brenda did not live in Romeo but would often come out to visit her parents who lived there. Over the years our friendship grew, and we became the best of friends but never entered into any type of dating relationship. Since Brenda was a little older than me, this meant she graduated from high school ahead of me. Brenda finished high school with honors, and then she joined the United States Army and headed off to basic training in Fort Jackson, South Carolina. I thought nothing of it at the time, and to be frank, I do not even remember her saying goodbye before she headed off to Fort Jackson. However, what I do remember is her return, and wow, what a return. One day that familiar face showed up back in Romeo, Florida. It was the girl next door. She had graduated from high school and joined the military. One day I was at her parents' house, and she showed up in uniform looking like a model for a U.S. Army poster. When I saw her, she was on leave from basic training while transitioning to her new duty station. Putting the beauty aside, the thing that I noticed was the fact that this uniform made her look important and proud. It was then that I realized my escape plan, and that plan was to drop out of high school and pursue a new path: the United States Army. I asked Brenda how she joined the Army, and she gave me her recruiter's business card; I proceeded to dial him up immediately. I told him what I wanted to do and how soon I wanted to do it. So, you guessed it: I soon dropped out of the eleventh grade and joined the military.

You see, I had long dreamed of being a truck driver (mechanical engineer) because I fell in love with the television show Moving On. Moving On was about two truck drivers who traveled throughout the country and had all kinds of amazing adventures. This reminded me of how I could escape my stepfather's wrath and hatred and find new adventures far from home. However, I had saw a recent Army recruiting commercial about mechanical engineers, so that is what I wanted to be – it was just that simple. I informed the Army recruiter and he said, "Great, come on in, take the Armed Services Vocational Aptitude Battery (ASVAB) test and we'll see if you qualify for a mechanical engineer job." For those of you who may be unfamiliar with the

ASVAB test, it includes tests in ten areas: general science (GS), arithmetic reasoning (AR), word knowledge (WK), paragraph comprehension (PC), mathematics knowledge (MK), electronics information (EI), auto information (AI), shop information (SI), mechanical comprehension (MC) and assembling objects (AO). Long story short, I did not have the ASVAB score I needed to qualify for the mechanical engineer job, so I ended up in combat arms as a cannon crew member. It did not matter to me, as long as I could escape my home life. Cannon crew member was the best course of action for me, so I said yes. However, there was a glitch in my escape plan that I did not see coming or anticipate. Since at the time I was only seventeen years old, I needed parental approval to enlist in the army. I cannot tell you how many days I spent tossing and turning pondering how I was going to approach my mom and get her to sign off on my application to join the military. Eventually, the day came when I approached my mother, and to this date, I cannot tell you what I said to mom, but apparently it was moving and inspirational enough because she pushed past her fears and signed my enlistment paperwork.

Afterwards I was given a report date of March 1980 which meant I only had a few months to remain in high school before I dropped out. When the time came, I dropped out of school and boarded a bus to the Military Entrance Processing (MEP) station in Jacksonville, Florida. From the MEP station I boarded an airplane for the first time in my life and headed to a place called Fort Sill, Oklahoma for basic training. This may sound strange, but I loved basic training. I was finally in a place where there was running water and no stepfather to curse me out at every turn. Mind you the drill sergeants did their share of cussing, but it was never personal. It was always for my improvement and not to bring me down. Interestingly enough, the drill sergeants were forever puzzled by my constant smile. Even in difficult circumstances and in spite of what they threw at me, I kept on smiling. What the drill sergeants did not realize is that my life was so much better than it was before I arrived at basic training. Plus, I knew no matter how much they threatened me with their cuss words they would never harm me, and that gave me comfort and joy. What I also realized in basic training is that if I did what the drill sergeants told me to do, I would be rewarded for my obedience. I mean, I had been obeying people all along, so this was no paradigm shift for me. Thus, I smiled at every turn, and it worked. I was soon promoted to acting sergeant and placed in charge of troops at which I was at a complete loss. During my time in basic training, I began to see and hear that I could excel at things in life. Take for example, growing up I used to always hang out on the school monkey bars because no one picked me to be on their basketball or football team. Well, as life would have it, when I entered the military, they had a physical event that included the monkey bars, and man, did I excel with great speed in navigating those bars. Additionally, I distinctly remember you had to complete the monkey bars before you could go into the

dining facility, or they would just send you back to the end of the line. Let me just say I was never sent to the back of the line, nor did I miss any meals. I completed my basic training, and it was not until many years later, after I requested my military records, that I discovered I had earned a letter for distinguished honor graduate in basic training.

> **Reverend G's Lesson for You**: *Sometimes you must smile even in the midst of the madness. Never let anyone dull the shine that God has put on your life.*

Classroom Again

I can tell you, personally, I never wanted to set foot in a classroom again once I was in the military. However, the company's first sergeant had a different plan. After I completed basic training at Fort Sill, Oklahoma, my first duty assignment was at a place called Fort Polk, Louisiana. When I arrived at Fort Polk, the company's first sergeant took one look at my record and said, "Private Gaines, go to the education center and sign up to complete your GED." Me, being a good soldier, followed his order reluctantly but quickly as directed. So, there I was: a high school dropout sitting in the education center working against my will to complete a diploma that I did not need or want (or so I thought at the time). However, I completed all the assignments, and by all accounts I did well, ultimately graduating with my GED in 1980. While this might seem a small achievement, it changed the trajectory of academics for many years to come. Completing my GED gave me a sense of accomplishment that I had never experienced before academically. While I regret dropping out of high school, one of my proudest moments is when they awarded me my GED. I never really had the chance to thank that first sergeant, but he put me on the road to success that I could never imagine at the time because it made me believe in myself; and that was something I had been missing for so exceptionally long.

> **Reverend G's Lesson for You:** *Please do not buy into your own self-doubt of your limited academic abilities. While learning comes easy for some people, you and I probably are the ones who have to work harder to understand the lesson, but it is all doable.*

How a Cold Day Changed the Course of My Life

There are some decisions made that can change the trajectory of one's life, and you may not even know it at the time the decision is made. I can assure you that I was not aware of the magnitude of my decision; I was simply trying literally to get out of the freezing weather. It happened back in the early '80s when I was stationed in West Germany during the time there was East and West Germany. My first overseas duty assignment in Germany was that of a field artillery man, hence the word "field." This meant I spent an awful lot of time in the field on training exercises and military maneuvers. This was not so bad during the spring and summer months, but the winter months can be brutal for a Florida boy who never really saw snow until he arrived in Europe. We were on an extended exercise, and I was nearly frozen after sitting on the cannon waiting for a fire mission. It was then I noticed this armored type of vehicle behind our firing position. I could see that there were soldiers sitting inside drinking hot coffee, playing cards, and just having a good ole time hanging out with each other. So of course, curiosity got the best of me. I walked over and asked them who they were and what they were doing because I wanted to know how to get that same type of job. They informed me that they were intelligence analysts, and it was their job to watch the battlefield from the confines of their warm armored vehicle. I quickly said to myself, "Note to Jeff; it's time for career change." After we returned to home base, I informed the unit's retention NCO that I wanted to change job description. He quickly said there were no positions available. While that saddened me, I later informed him that if the job was not available, I would be leaving the military altogether. To my amazement, an abbreviated time later he came back and offered me the intelligence analyst position with a class date and a follow assignment to a place in the desert called Fort Huachuca, Arizona. So, it was without delay that I went from a particularly important war-fighting mission to another important mission that would allow me to stay warm during the winter. This decision was nothing more than an attempt to avoid winter weather, but this fateful decision opened so many different doors for me that I do not think were available to me in my current role as a cannon crewman. I departed Germany and headed to Fort Huachuca, Arizona. There I spent several months learning a new tradecraft and enjoying all of the beautiful sunshine that Arizona had to offer. From that launch pad I found myself in a host of intelligence positions in a variety of army assignments overseas, and in the Washington, DC area.

> **Reverend G's Lesson for You:** *Do not be afraid to ask questions, you never know where their answers may take you.*

Academia Nirvana at the Defense Intelligence College.

There are people who can see you doing bigger things in life than you can see for yourself. Case in point, while stationed at Fort Huachuca, Arizona as a staff sergeant at the Intelligence School and Center, an announcement came out that the Defense Intelligence College was accepting applications for its undergraduate intelligence program . I produced all kinds of reasons why I was not ready or qualified for the program; in short, I was afraid of rejection. However, I had worked with someone on staff, and she approached me about submitting my application for the intelligence program. I gave her all the aforementioned excuses, which she quickly shot full of holes and almost ordered me to submit my application. She did not stop there; she actually helped me fill out the paperwork and reviewed my entire packet for accuracy. I submitted my application and waited for the inevitable rejection, but to my surprise I was accepted for a full-ride scholarship. This school was located in the Washington, DC area, which meant the entire family had to relocate with me. Mind you, in my mind, from an intelligence professional perspective, the Defense Intelligence College was the crème de la crème of military schools – at least that is my humble unbiased opinion. Upon receiving the news, I could not wait to thank my colleague who had encouraged me to apply. I attended the program and graduated, which led to various levels of assignments within my career. Over the years I tried to find my colleague but was never able to connect with her once I left Fort Huachuca. So, Janet, if you ever read this book, I cannot thank you enough for how you pushed me out of my comfort zone and changed the trajectory of my intelligence career.

Being Fired from My First Dream Job – It Hurt Like Hell

As an enlisted member of the US armed forces, one's dream is to always climb to the top of the enlisted ranks, culminating at the E-9 level (Sergeant Major/Command Sergeant Major). However, generally speaking, in order to hit that level you must have a leadership position at the E-8 level as a first sergeant. For me, reaching E-9 is what I lived and breathed for every day of my career. In my mind I worked hard and was placed in various leadership positions from E4 – E7. So, I cannot tell you how thrilled I was when I was informed that I was selected to be a first sergeant for an intelligence organization in the Washington, DC area. I was literally walking on cloud nine, well, maybe not literally but you get my point. I loved working for the soldiers and watching them overcome challenges and achieve their dreams with promotions, awards, and special assignments. In particular, although I am not an enthusiastic fan of social events, as the first sergeant, I loved the formal dining events where we would all dress up in our finest US Army uniforms and just have fun eating and drinking; yes, it did involve alcohol. For me, there was no greater job that I had ever experienced that compared to being a first sergeant. Things only became better when I was also informed

that I was selected to attend the first sergeant course. By far, the first sergeant course knocked my attendance at the Defense Intelligence College off the peddle. The day came for me to head to the airport and fly off to attend the course in Texas. However, before I could leave the house my commanding officer called me and said the higher ups had decided that I was not the person they wanted in the job. They informed me that they were not only cancelling my class attendance, but they were removing me from the first sergeant position.

I can still remember it like it was yesterday. This hit me like an airbag deployed during an accident, and after I hung up the phone, I cried like a baby, not just that day, but for the days that followed. My wife became concerned that I was entering a state of depression. Needless to say, when you are in a leadership role and you are removed, they do not leave you in the same organization because it can cause all kinds of complications. It was then that I learned that they were sending me to an office that did not know they were getting me – what I like to refer to as the broken toy.

I went there with much apprehension to meet my new boss, and I am sure he had just as many concerns as I did since he was not told I was arriving to work for him. So, the time came for me to meet my new boss, Larry. I met him in the foyer of the building and we talked, and he explained what his role was and what he was looking to do with someone with my skillset. I of course explained my situation and we agreed to move forward with my assignment to his office. While I went there with a heavy heart and a great dislike for how the army had treated me, he was able to look beyond that drama and put me straight to work. Once I started working for him, I quickly realized he was one of the best civilian bosses I had ever worked for, plus we had all kinds of connections. We were both from Florida, loved sports cars, and craved boiled peanuts; if you are not from the South, you may not get the boiled peanut thing. Anyway, he began to mentor me in a manner that was focused on my future and not just the task at hand. We used to travel together for business presentations, but after a few trips, Larry began to send me on brief solo trips to organizations with the opportunity to make decisions. Larry was not only my boss and mentor – he ultimately became and is still my friend. He literally saved my life from a disastrous firing to a position that offered a better transition to life outside the military. I would ultimately retire from Larry's shop with a nice send-off and a prestigious medal to go with it.

However, the story with Larry does not end there. To my surprise, after being in the private sector for a year, I received a call from Larry. "Are you ready to come home?" he asked. "What do you mean?" "I have a GS13 position available if you are willing to apply and pass the interviews." I, of course, said I was ready. Since I did not know anything about working as a federal employee, Larry took the time to teach me how to dress and negotiate my salary. I followed his instructions to the T and was successful at winning the GS13

Intelligence Specialist position. This was huge for me because it meant I did not have to start at one of the lower grades and work my way up the food chain. The even bigger surprise when I arrived at Larry's office as a federal employee, he had reserved the same desk and phone number that I had when I was on active duty in the United States Army. I was able to jump right back into the swing of things and spent several years working for Larry. Even after I moved on to other assignments, Larry and I stayed in contact. He helped me get into other organizations and was by far my best reference for years. To date, Larry and I are still in contact some twenty plus years later, and just recently in 2021, he and I had breakfast at First Watch in Lakewood Ranch catching up on old times.

> **Reverend G's Lesson for You:** *Sometimes serious stuff does happen to good people; what will you do when it happens to you? I hope that you persevere beyond temporary setbacks.*

A New Life in the Private Sector then Government Service

To someone who is unfamiliar with military life and what it means when you leave the military, this section may be hard to connect with, so allow me to walk you through what it means to approach a new life in the private sector and then with the federal government. First, please understand that I joined the military at the youthful age of seventeen, and it was the first time I had ever left home and found myself surrounded by strangers of all different ethnicities and backgrounds. What one quickly learns is that the military is not just a job, it is a calling, a new life that is completely different from the one to which you are accustomed. The longer you are in the military, the farther you travel from the old life and the more you see the world through the military lens. If you listen to orders and work hard, you can succeed in the military. With that success comes promotions and relocations to places around the globe. Technically, you never have to worry about a job because you receive orders and basically show up at your next duty station with a position waiting for you. So, imagine doing this for twenty years, never really having to worry about a job to where you are leaving the military and have to compete with others, go in for interviews and negotiate your salary, which prior to this was unheard of. When it came time to leave the military, it was quite a daunting task which caused a lot of fear and anxiety within me. I found myself intimidated by the process to the extent that I had to join a military transition group to assist me. I distinctly remember during the transition class they required us to come dressed in business attire as though we were going in for an interview. I found my best army shoes and the most hideous black tie for the occasion. I was judged by my peers and the facilitator, not

in a bad way, but in a manner that informed me that I did not look like the success I was seeking. From that encounter I knew I needed help and sought out a mentor who taught me how to dress the part. Thank you, Larry. Dressing is only one aspect of many when it comes to transitioning to the private sector. The one key aspect is salary negotiations, which is something you never had to worry about in the military. I mean, your salary was posted in the newspapers, so everyone knew exactly what you made. Of course, this is completely different in the private sector. Before I proceed, please take into consideration that I started my transition long before we had smart phones and apps to help us with salary determination. This part of the transition was critical because if I accepted a job with too low of a salary, it would set the tone for future jobs because most companies wanted to know your current salary before making you an offer. Of course, this practice is no longer acceptable in today's world, but back then, it was a widespread practice, at least in my experience. That being said, I was able to negotiate my first job salary much higher than I could imagine. Little did I know, it would turn out to be one of the worst jobs I ever had in my life. In short, I learned that going for the money alone is not the best approach to accepting a respectable job offer. However, I was able to leave that job after several months and found a job at the Pentagon for the office of Secretary of Defense. I loved the company I worked for and the people I worked with. But it was a struggle for me to fit in because I missed the structure and comradeship of working for the military, so I longed to go back to that lifestyle. And then one day I received a call that changed the trajectory of my private sector career. It was Larry offering me a job back at my former place of duty.

> **Reverend G's Lesson for You:** *Transition can be tough, but if you talk with the right people, they will help you get through the process.*

Assignments to United States Spy Agencies

You may be asking the question: why is an ordained preacher talking about working for spy agencies? Well, the short answer is up until this point in my life, I had never worked full time in the church, which means I had a full-time job working for the federal government. I have had some amazing opportunities in my life, but when I landed my first job working in the intelligence community, I felt like the black 007. Putting all jokes aside, it was a humbling and amazing experience to work to help protect this great nation we live in called the land of the free and home of the brave. So, let there be no doubt, I love the flag, and will proudly salute the flag every chance I get to do so. While the jobs I had were exciting, not all of them, though most of them were the best part about my career in the intelligence community. The best thing was the fact that those with whom I worked constituted the most diverse group of people I had a chance to work alongside. These professionals came from all aspects of life: different religious backgrounds, different sexual orientations, and a host of varying academic achievements. While many of my jobs were great, I would have to say my last job in the federal government was by far my best assignment.

My last assignment was in an organization called the Financial Crimes Enforcement Network aka FinCEN. The reason it was my best assignment is because I had no financial experience in my background and was hired for my leadership and people skill abilities alone. This meant I had an uphill climb from day one, a challenge which I loved, and my boss at the time was open to innovative ideas and new ways of doing things. Needless to say, over the course of my assignment at FinCEN, I learned so much about financial transactions that I never knew existed. Additionally, I had this amazing opportunity to

build an office from the ground up and was there long enough to actually see it become operational; sometimes this is a rarity in life. I also worked with so many amazing people that did not come from the same career path as I had, which gave us the opportunity to learn from each other. Truth be known, when my assignment time at FinCEN was up and it was time for me to go back to the mothership, I could not bring myself to accept the idea that I might have to go back and do what I was doing prior to my assignment and FinCEN. At this time, I decided to put in my retirement papers and move on to a new exciting chapter.

Reverend G's Lesson for You: *Do not be afraid to take on new opportunities even though you have no experience in that field of expertise.*

Attending Seminary – A Thirst to Learn More

For so many years I had a thirst to learn more about the Word of God, not just at my local church but at a recognized institution of higher learning. I had a master's in public administration, and it helped me land better and higher paying jobs in the private sector. So likewise, I thought a master's in theology would help me preach better, teach better, and yes, land a job in full-time ministry. You see, full-time ministry was something I always longed for. I wanted to work for God and not have to split my attention by being bi-vocational, meaning part time church and full time for someone else or some organization. To this end I set down a path of finding a university that could scratch my itch. While doing my research it dawned on me that my son had attended a Christian university in Lynchburg, Virginia, and by all accounts, he had a wonderful experience. So, I thought it would be an honor to attend the same university my son attended. From there I put all the required paperwork together, including letters of recommendations from various clergy friends, and sent my package off to the university. It seemed like an eternity, but I waited for what I knew was just a rubber stamp "you are accepted" letter. I mean, for what reason would a Christian college reject a minister of the Gospel? Well, as you guessed it, they denied my application without providing me an explanation. Well, I am not the type to just sit back and let people tell me what I cannot do without at least giving me an explanation. I proceeded to email and call, and I received a reply pretty much saying I was not the type of student they wanted in their program. I mean, I was shocked, angry, and downright frustrated with this university. However, I have learned that once you rush through all of those emotions, you are still facing the old question of what is next. To be honest, I had not considered any other university because I just knew I was a sure winner for this university. So, I really had to start from ground zero again. After much research and talking with others, I learned of a university called Regent University in Virginia Beach. Long story short, I applied and was accepted into their practical theology program. I must tell you it was the best learning experience I have ever had in any college or university. The opportunity to learn theology from the great minds of the university and those of my classmates was truly exceptional.

> **Reverend G's Lesson for You:** *My friends, when life throws you rejection, do not give up. God has other opportunities in store for you.*

Accepting Orders from My Wife the CEO

Life lesson: marriage is a partnership not a dictatorship. Over the years I have been asked what it is like working for my wife all the time. I would jokingly say I have been working for her all these years so nothing has changed. But the reality of our new dynamic is that it did not start off easy. In fact, it was quite bumpy, and to be quite honest with you, I did not know if the whole work-for-your-spouse thing was going to work for us as a couple. Early on, Brenda would tell me I was fired, and I can remember hearing that at least eight times. However, me being the competitive person, I told her I quit at least nine times. I think married couples who work together or work for each other have a unique opportunity to grow their marriage beyond the business. What I mean is this: we both learned that marriage is a partnership and not a dictatorship. My job is to partner with Brenda on her dreams and goals and support them as much as I possibly can. Here is what I had to learn about our company, and it may or may not apply to your company or marriage. But here is what I did: I recognize, accept, and respect that my wife is the CEO of the company. While I may have disagreements about some of her decisions, nonetheless, they are her decisions to make. If I were working for some Fortune 500 company and disagreed with their decisions, I can guarantee you I would not be in their bedroom arguing about policy decisions. No, my friend, I would conclude that it was their company, and they get to run it as they want to run it. Sometimes they would listen to my input but most times not so much. Therefore, do likewise with your spouse. But conversely if you are the person that your spouse is working for, please be careful not to over-extend spouse versus boss rules. Additionally, the key to remember is that your spouse is choosing to work for you, and in my book, that is a huge show of respect and honor. Furthermore, I do not know if we could have done this early on in our marriage because we were still trying to figure out who we were, let alone who to work for, so proceed with prayer and caution. Whatever the case, it can be such a rewarding experience to know you are working on something together and building a better future for your family.

> **Reverend G's Lesson for You:** *Equal partners in business with defined roles, but the sanctity of the marriage triumph everything.*

Worst Church Job Offer Ever - What a Let Down

In a previous section I mentioned my attendance at seminary and what an amazing experience that was for me. What I did not go into detail is why I wanted to go to seminary in the first place. Well, for me I have never had the opportunity to be fully employed by a church. Mind you, I have done a lot of volunteer work for churches. I always had a desire to find full-time employment at any church that would hire me. I wanted to know what it was like to be able to open my Bible at my desk and not have someone look at me and file a grievance. I wanted to know what it was like to prepare for a sermon every day and not be interrupted with mundane tasks by people who did not give a hill of beans about me. From this perspective I began to look for church jobs that I was interested in, only to find that most, if not all, required a formal theology-based degree. So, the light came on and I concluded that I needed to go to seminary to be competitive for church jobs. Yes, I wanted to improve my knowledge and preaching skills, but in all transparency, I wanted a full-time church position title. So, I cannot tell you how thrilled I was when one night my pastor called me out the blue and informed me that the church had a vacancy. He thought I would be a great candidate and wanted to know if I was interested in the position. After I heard what the position was about, I felt like it was the job I had been praying for, and the icing on the cake was the fact that it was with the church I was currently a member of and had been for many years. We also discussed an agreed upon salary with the interviews to follow. I was puzzled that I had been working there for free for nearly twenty years doing all kinds of ministry work but had to do an interview for the position. But I concluded maybe it was just a formality. I was excited and informed my family and a few close friends, and of course they were excited for me. During the course of time, I had given the church my start date and commenced to relinquish my roles in our family-owned business. I went to a couple of interviews and seemingly passed them with flying colors. But something struck me as odd. I noticed that people I spoke to every Sunday who worked on programs with me never mentioned the job or congratulated me for being considered for the position. However, I pushed past this information, assuming they were told to keep things closely held. Well, months went by, and I finally reached the date in which I informed the pastor that I could start. I saw him pretty much every Sunday in the back office where all the preachers would gather before service. He never mentioned the job to me or where we were in the process. So, I sent him an email informing him of my start date and wanted to know what I needed to do to begin the process. I mean, Brenda was already buying items to decorate my church office. Well, to my shock and disbelief, I received an email from him indicating he had not made a decision, so no start date or in-processing was provided. After reading that email, I realized I had made that tragic mistake of thinking I had the job before I actually had the job. I had already completed a twenty-year interview of working for free for this church, so what could be the issue? After receiving that email, I quickly went back to my professional way of

thinking about new jobs, and that is if they treat you this way bringing you onboard, do you really think it will get any better once you arrive? I think not. I then proceeded to reestablish the responsibilities I had within our family-owned business with a mindset that if the pastor calls or does not call it was not an issue for me any longer. Well, months went by, and again I saw him on a regular weekly basis with no proof of job offers.

Then one day out of nowhere the pastor called to inform me that he was offering me the job. Well, so much time and drama had passed that I was no longer excited or amazed about the opportunity. I thanked him but respectfully declined the position. He asked me to take a few days to reconsider the offer and I reluctantly agreed. We had a call a few days later at which time I declined the position a second time and concluded the call rather abruptly. For me, this was a change moment. I recognized he could be my pastor, but he could or would not be my boss, and to me there is an absolute difference. Additionally, this awful job offer left an unpleasant experience in the eyes of my children and close friends, and they felt he had disrespected me and my relationship with that particular church. I personally will tell you I never saw him in the same light or held him to high esteem as I did before this lousy decision process to hire me. In looking back, I have met hiring managers that did not even know me, and in the space of twenty minutes they decided on the spot to hire me. Here I was twenty years on a volunteer basis, and it took months to get a decision, and this only happened at my prodding. Worst job offer ever.

> **Reverend G's Lesson for You:** *An excellent job with a poor boss is never a good thing. Good boss with a poor job, well, that is doable. Bad leadership is just bad leadership; it does not get better with time, so do not waste your time hanging out with people who do not value or respect who you are as a person.*

Relationships, They Are Complicated

Early Relationship Failures as a Teenager

It is understood that if you are poor and have lousy clothing, no self-respecting girl wants to hang around you, and that was me. I never had any dates early in high school, never received Valentine's cards, nor was I invited to a dance party at my local school. Even if I were invited, I would not have gone just for sheer fear of being embarrassed or bullied. I did manage to connect with girls in the Central Florida area who did not know all of my story. However, when you do not have a father figure around to help you navigate these relationships, they often end in disaster, and mine were no exception. So, I did manage to date a few girls, but the word date might be an overstatement. Then one day I was introduced to a young lady who stole my heart, and I fell head over heels for her. In my mind, she felt the same way. However, I had to depart for the military, so we wrote and called each other. I thought our love was strong, if there is such a thing at age seventeen. However, when basic training was over, I wanted to surprise her and not tell her I was coming home, so I decided to drop by her house unannounced with some of my childhood friends along with me. Well, to my surprise, I knocked on the door, rushed in, and there she was sitting on the sofa with her new boyfriend. She did not acknowledge me or my presence. I was devastated, and it took everything within me to keep from breaking down right there in the living room. I managed to keep it together long enough to get outside, only to cry like a newborn baby. Of course, the fellas that were with me had no mercy and teased me about being dumped in such a painful fashion. If I were them, I would have probably done the same thing. I left there heartbroken, determined to never let a woman steal my heart. Overall, I handled it very badly and it took a toll on me and the several relationships that followed.

> **Reverend G's Lesson for You:** *It is okay to love, but for those who are young in age, do not give all until you know all, and to know all will take time. Trust me on this one; you have time, so slow your roll.*

Falling in Love with the Girl Next Door

Earlier I mentioned Brenda and how we were good friends but never really dated. However, I did take special notice of her after the uniform appearance. She eventually left and headed to Fort Carson, Colorado, while I eventually ended up at Fort Polk, Louisiana. We stayed in contact via letters and the occasional call. Our friendship at the time never matured to the point of dating because neither one of us saw each other that way. We were simply good friends who would sit on the hood of her parents' car and talk about what we dreamed of doing in the future. But let me tell you about the day that all changed. One day I was back in Florida on military leave and so was Brenda. Our military leaves were not coordinated, but we just happened to both be home visiting our parents and ran into each other. After that encounter we decided to go out for dinner and a movie, and after the movie we found ourselves not wanting to depart from each other's company. I remember the first kiss and the first hug of passion like it was yesterday. From that moment we were inseparable (except for military assignments of course). Then a strange thing happened. Brenda decided that she no longer wanted to be in the military, and I received an assignment to Fort Stewart, Georgia which meant I could be home in Florida every weekend, although I was home on a frequent basis. Through these visits I fell madly in love with the girl next door and prayed that God would make her my wife. I can remember stressing that I was 'overspending' $175 for a diamond ring because I had never spent that much money on any girlfriend before Brenda.

Unlike today's world, I did not want to make a big engagement announcement because I truly did not know if she would say yes or no. I did not want to be embarrassed. So, the night arrived, and I leaned down on one knee in her sister's apartment, asking her to be my wife. She said yes, and I was so relieved to place the ring on her finger. I immediately drove to her parents' home to ask her father for his daughter's hand. Her father saw the ring on Brenda's finger and asked where the diamond was. We all laughed, and he gave his blessing for me to marry his daughter. We had planned to marry on Brenda's birthday in December, but when I received orders for an overseas assignment, we moved our wedding date to July.

> **Reverend G's Lesson for You:** *Sometimes the person that is right for you is the person that is staring you right in face and you do not know it at the time.*

A Bumpy Start After a Nice Honeymoon

Brenda and I had a double wedding ceremony with her sister and now brother-in law. It was a beautiful wedding at the little church in Dunnellon, Florida which is still there today. My brother Wilbert was my best man and her father Herman walked both of his daughters down the aisle. We had a nice reception in her parents' backyard in Romeo, Florida, and the wedding was well attended by family and friends. From there we went on a honeymoon trip to Orlando, Florida where we stayed at a nice little hotel called Howard Johnson.

During this time, I was not aware that there were family members that did not want Brenda to marry me because of my social economic status. Thank God she followed her heart and had encouragement from her parents. We left the honeymoon knowing that I had to head back to Fort Stewart, Georgia and that we would be separated for a while. To people who say separations make the heart grow fonder, I say, truly BS. Separation makes young people lustful and makes it easier to fall into temptation, so thanks be to God our separation was not that long. We ultimately ended up in Illesheim, West Germany within our first six months of marriage and it was a godsend. I say that to say this: If we had not gone to Germany to be completely on our own, I do not know if we would have made it through the first two years of our marriage. There was a time in Germany when Brenda wanted to leave me, and there was a time when I wanted to leave Brenda. Fortunately, there was never a time when we wanted to leave each other at the same time. I know that was a mouthful. Additionally, being in Germany meant we really had to depend on each other, and we could not just walk out and leave; what a lifesaver that was for our marriage. We muddled through the first three years of marriage bickering and blaming each other for self-imposed drama. We went to counseling with a member of the local church and that was an immense help. We also had parents who did not choose sides, they chose issues, so right or wrong was determined through your decision-making and not your family heritage.

Reverend G's Lesson for You: *I think family members' involvement in a marriage is a good thing; however, too much family involvement can be disastrous. Married folks: please love each other, be patient with each other, correct each other, but most importantly forgive each other.*

Looking Back on 37 Years of Marriage

Proverbs 18:22 states that "he who finds a wife finds a good thing and obtains favor with the Lord." I would flat out be lying if I told you I started our marriage with this verse as the backdrop of wedded bliss. No, my friend, it was pretty much the exact opposite when we started. Allow me to again go back in time to when I was about five years old. My mom and dad physically separated, and we moved to a place called Romeo, Florida which caused so many ups and downs in my life; I would need several more books to write it and a good bottle of scotch. As life would have it, one day I was on military leave back home in Romeo and I stopped by her mom's house to say hello to her parents. There she was, all grown up and looking more beautiful than when I  first saw her at age five. We were genuinely happy to see each other that day and made a date to go out for dinner later that evening. I still remember it clear as day. Red Lobster was our place and continues to be one of our favorites even until this day. We had a wonderful time at dinner, and I think we both knew from that point that we had similar dreams and goals which led to more dates, culminating into a wedding in 1984 in Dunnellon, Florida.

We are now approaching our 38th wedding anniversary, and I would like to tell you that it has been an easy road but that would be far from the truth. In fact, we have had our challenges, bumpy roads, and meaningless arguments interspersed with fulfilling moments of great love and joy for each other. But I can tell you that I am a blessed man for I have truly married the woman of my dreams. What we have learned over all these years is to try and get behind each other's dreams as much as possible, even if it means putting our own dreams on hold for a while. Yes, sacrifice for the greater good, for the betterment of the family. I will say this: some may slam the book, but a woman who submits herself to her husband as outlined in Ephesians 5:22 will gain a husband that will do what Christ did for the church, give his life. Yes, a married couple that honors God's Word will obtain great blessings. I did not come to this conclusion on our honeymoon night, and neither did Brenda. No, my friend, it is and will always continue to be a work in progress. Marriage is never easy, and it requires continued blood, sweat, and tears. I mean, sure, you could go at this thing haphazardly, but we know where that will ultimately end up.

Let me be completely transparent, we both entered our marriage at an early age. We had not even figured out who we were or what we really wanted in life. That being said, with the help of parents, family, friends, and the church, we survived some really rocky roads. To be honest, I do not know if we could have made it on our own. I personally think the biggest step to our success was not of our choosing. No, it was actually the military. Brenda had completed her time in the military before we were married so she knew what military life was like. It was no surprise that I came down with orders to relocate to Germany. This meant that we were married in July, and I was headed to Germany in December with Brenda arriving in January. Being across the ocean thousands of miles away from home meant that we really had to depend on each other for survival and comfort, and that is just what we did. It meant that whenever there was an argument we could not just get in the car and go home. No, we had to work it out. Please remember this was long before the internet and cell phones, so you were reduced to writing letters, and by the time you received a response, the crisis was over or well beyond the point of advice from friends.

Those three years overseas caused us to really learn about each other and the duties of a husband and wife. You see, I did not come into this marriage with an example of what it was like being a good husband. For me as a man, my mom's relationship with my stepfather ended up not being a good example to follow, and my birth father had moved on many years before Brenda and I even met each other. In other words, I was learning on the fly, so the turbulence was frequent and long. However, the tide began to turn when we ended up in Arizona for a few years. While our first child was born in Germany, our second child was born in Fort Huachuca, Arizona. This just made us closer as a couple because we both loved kids, especially our children. It was during this time that I made an effort to always date my wife. This meant I would plan a day trip to local cities and spend the night. We did not have much money, but the little we did have we made the best of. These dates continue even to this day. What I have learned over all these years is that I still do not know everything about Brenda, and I am willing to learn as we go through various stages in our lives.

Reverend G's Lesson for You: *In my experience I have seen couples work harder on the wedding date than the marriage. There is a difference. Weddings last a few hours but a good marriage that can stand the test of time can last a lifetime. The catch is you have to work hard to make it last.*

Me and the Church

Me a Preacher – Climbing Mount Everest

As a child, going to church was never an option. My mom made us get dressed and go to Sunday school and church with a big smile on our faces. So, when I left home and struck out on my own, I vowed that I  would avoid church at all costs and was successful in my avoidance approach for several years. However, the woman I married never gave up on her commitment to attend church and serve the Lord. I never tried to change that as long as she did not try to force me into attending church, and she never did. However, what I have learned is when God has a plan for you, you can run but you cannot hide. The very first apartment my wife and I had was on the top floor in a building with no elevator. God being God had a couple living right below us in a similar apartment, and it just so happened he was a pastor of a local church. Brenda loved this connection; however, I tried to avoid them at all costs. But sometimes you just cannot get away from what God has in store for you.

Brenda started attending their church and would come back all excited, talking about the moving of the Holy Spirit. Mind you, I was still working through my stepdaddy issues, not to mention the struggles of newlyweds, so I wanted to know why she was so happy. I decided to attend church, and wow, what a difference it made in my life. I stood before Pastor Watson and the church and gave my life to Jesus. From there I served as an usher, a deacon, and ultimately became the pastor's aide. I was thrilled to be in the presence and gain from the experience of this godly man. Pastor Watson taught me a lot in church, but the best learning came when I would drive him to various locations in Germany and he would impart wisdom and knowledge to me on a one-on-one basis.

What I have not mentioned up to this point is that I am an introvert. My wife might even say I am an extreme introvert combined with a fear of speaking. I could never imagine where this "accepting the Lord" gig was going to take me, but I followed God's teaching and we eventually ended up in a small gospel church in Fort Huachuca, Arizona. There I was given the responsibility of teaching and was occasionally asked to speak to the congregation during various church events. Somehow this did not fill the void of servitude. I felt the Lord tugging at my heart telling me I needed to do more and that He wanted to me to preach the gospel. I fought this internal struggle for what seemed like an eternity. After making many excuses, all of which were shot down by my loving wife, people in the church, and our Lord's conviction, with reluctance I accepted this call to ministry.

That was not the difficult part. The difficult part was telling Pastor McCaa, my pastor at the time, that I had this call, and figuring out how to explain it to him. I mustered up the courage and went to talk with him. To my amazement he asked me what took me so long to accept this and that he was waiting for me to step forward. Man, what a relief that was. Pastor McCaa then began to tell me how I would attend training and he would mentor me for at least twelve months before I would preach to the congregation. After hearing this, I was ecstatic to know I would not have to stand up and preach for twelve months. It just made my day until one day I decided to visit a friend in California.

When God called me to the ministry, our son was our only child at the time, and he and I spent a lot of time together hanging out doing guy stuff. Well, I decided he and I would take a road trip from Arizona to California to have a father-son bonding experience and it was amazing. We arrived there in California, and Tim, the friend I was visiting, was a church musician/director. Tim invited me to his church for a gospel concert, and wow, what a great worship experience. However, through word of mouth they found out that I was a preacher and wanted me to preach at this church in two nights' time. Of course, I could not let my friend down, so I agreed. Mind you, my plan was to not preach for twelve months, so I had not developed any sermon outlines. I needed to pull something together rather quickly. Red flag! I was in a state of panic and the time to preach drew nearer. Wait, it gets better. To my amazement I was not the only preacher. There were several of us in the lineup and I was praying they would run out of time and say they needed to invite me back at a later date, but that did not happen. I was like number four on the list and was watching these amazing preachers stand up and give electrifying sermons. The congregation was on fire with their responses and plenty of amens. Then to top matters off, number three in the line–you know the guy right before

me— received a standing ovation. And then they called my name. I looked at the stairs leading to the pulpit, and they looked like a climb up Mount Everest. I made the long journey up those gigantic seven steps and stood there in front of this standing room-only congregation and began to open my mouth.

Let me just tell you, I was horrible and really stunk up the place. I fumbled my words and was so nervous I nearly passed out. There was this one part of the sermon where I was supposed to say the houses we live in and the cars we drive, but I said was the houses we drive and cars we live in, and it just went downhill from there. The congregation, knowing that I was trying my best, was exceedingly kind to try and cheer me on, but I could not see it or feel it. I just wanted to climb back down Mount Everest and hide for the remainder of the event. Strangely enough, I still remember the subject of that sermon, "God's Word Never Changes." My friend could not resist teasing me about the house and car mix up, but the subject stuck so much, I remember hearing kids walking around saying mockingly, "God's Words Never Changes." That was my very first sermon as a preacher, and what I learned from that experience is that you must always be ready to preach at any given time. Pastor McCaa taught me to always have a sermon printed and tucked into the back of my Bible, so when you get these short notices you can refresh and go forward with clarity and courage, and, yes, I did that for many years. However, I thank God for the internet and shared drive; now I can access a library of sermons at any given time. As I reflected back on that date over the years, I was timid about preaching that sermon subject again at any other churches for fear I might botch it again. But one day I sensed the courage to preach that sermon nearly twenty-six years later. I texted my friend Tim and asked him to stream it from his home in Texas. I preached the sermon in Northern Virginia. After I finished preaching "God's Word Never Changes II," he texted me with the words: "the houses we drive and cars we live in lol, love you Tim." He further told me that he had the video of that sermon from twenty-six years ago and was going to load it onto YouTube. Of course, he was joking. This was how my calling into the ministry started on the climb of Mount Everest.

Loss of Loved Ones – Absolute Madness

When people hear that your loved one has died, they say things like they "understand," and they "feel your pain." No, they do not, so please shut up and just stand with me and keep your big mouth closed. I know that sounds harsh but what I mean is this: To all the people to whom I have uttered those words, I meant well but I apologize. I did not realize what I was saying, please forgive me. Allow me to explain my revelation of the unintentional pain I may have caused you.

In 2007 I received a call that my sister Bernadette aka "Bunny" was in the hospital, so I decided to call her and see how she was doing. Bunny said, "Jeff, I am doing okay, and the hospital is going to release me tomorrow." We said our niceties and hung up the phone. The next thing I knew is that the phone rang with a family member telling me that Bunny had died of heart failure. I cannot even begin to tell you how devastated I was to hear this news. To this day, I still cannot remember what I did during the months after Bunny's death. It was not until eight months later, when I was starting to adjust to losing Bunny that I received a call in October from my mom telling me she was in the ambulance headed to have gallbladder surgery. Again, I thought nothing of it. However, when the surgeons performed the surgery, they could not stop the bleeding which meant my mom slipped into a coma-like state for months. I traveled back and forth from Virginia to Florida praying and hoping that my mom would pull through, and then I received that call on December 30 informing me that my mom had passed away.

From that point forward my life took a dive into darkness and despair. I went into a fog and did not know how I was going to come out of it. In a span of less than twelve months I had lost two of the most significant ladies in my life. This is why I started this chapter off with the fact that people do not know what they are saying when they tell you they understand your loss. I had done the same thing, because I truly did not understand the grip of grief and its devastating impact until I experienced my own personal losses. Yes, I had said those cliché words hoping to console someone, but in the end, I probably offended them or caused them more grief. To this I say, I am terribly sorry; I did not understand the true depth of your pain and grief.

> **Reverend G's Lesson for You:** *When assisting others in grief, what you do is far better than what you say, so please work hard to keep your lips sealed and ears open.*

Coming Apart with Grief

To start this section off let me say: if you have never experienced grief then I recommend you skip this section completely. This begs the question, why would I make such a drastic statement to my valuable readers? Well, it is like this, I will be saying things about losing a loved one that only someone who has truly experienced the madness of grief can understand and appreciate. So, let us dive into coming apart with grief. There is nothing on earth that compares to losing someone you love. Yes, divorce is hard, but I do not think it

is a fair comparison to losing someone you love whom you will never be able to touch or laugh with for the rest of your life. Losing a job, and dare I say it, losing a beloved family pet, does not compare to losing a human being, so please do not allow anyone to convince you otherwise. Do not get me wrong, the aforementioned losses are painful and can catastrophically impact one's life. But let me tell you what grief does; it takes you to places that you have probably never dreamed of in your worst nightmare. It can cause your mind and heart to play awful tricks on you, well, at least for me it did. When I lost my mom, my whole life just came apart. I felt like it all was over for me. Yes, I was forty-five years old at the time, but it felt like I was a child. This was the person that not only gave me life but sustained me through life, to whom I owed my very own life. I can tell you I had a complete shutdown functionally as a human being. Even though I cannot put a specific timeframe on how long I was unconsciously dealing with grief, I can say it was a period of months which seemed like decades to me. I could not answer phone calls. I could not muster up enough strength to exercise, which of course led to weight gain. Ultimately it affected my sleep, resulting in having the doctor prescribe sleeping medication. Yes, my dear friends, I was a hot mess and coming apart at the seams with no light at the end of the tunnel. You might ask why I am sharing such transparent details about my grief. The answer is this: if you are experiencing grief, know that you are not alone, and I want to encourage you to seek help from your family, friends, doctors, and the church.

> **Reverend G's Lesson for You:** *Grief is maddening, but you are not alone, so please seek help from a friend or a professional counselor.*

Stepping Down from the Church Means Doing More

I have been preaching and working in various roles in the church for over thirty years, and I personally cannot remember ever a time that I was not engaged in some type of demanding role; from interim pastor to youth pastor, usher, deacon, or Sunday school teacher. But there comes a time in one's life when you need to take care of yourself before you can take care of others. This is exactly where I ended up; but mind you not of my own decision or revelation. What that means is that others did a direct intervention on me without my knowledge, but that is how these direct interventions occur. Here is how my intervention went down.

I covered the subject of grief in the previous section. I was still coming apart months afterward, but I did not know just how bad I was falling apart. Oh, do not get me wrong, my lovely wife of over thirty years was telling me, but her kind words fell on deaf ears. No, my friend, it was not until one day I was sitting up in the pulpit of the church during a rather joyous service when members of the church approached me at the altar. I was thinking they wanted me to pray for them but that was not the case. They gathered around me and said that they wanted to tell me something. I was there with open ears because they were all members of the singles ministry of which Brenda and I were the leaders at the time. They told me in a most loving way that they appreciated me so much for serving in the singles ministry through the loss of my mother, but it was time for me to take a break. In other words, it was time for me to step down and get the healing I needed. If I were a man of tears, I would have broken down right there on the spot, but I did not because that is not the way I roll. However, after reflecting on their words and the words of my wife, I came to a hard decision that it was time for me to not only step down from the singles ministry but all the ministries in which I was involved. I desperately needed to take some time to heal and process my grief. So that is exactly what I did for about twelve months. By the time I decided to jump back into things, I can tell you I had benefitted from the much-needed break and time of reflection.

> **Reverend G's Lesson for You:** *You do not have to carry the weight of the world on your shoulder on a full-time basis. I recommend you switch to part time or a 1099. In this fashion someone else can take care of the load. It worked for me, and I believe it will work for you.*

Cancer Scare and Panic Mode

Life Lesson: it is easy to tell people to trust in God when they have a medical scare, but panic can overtake you when it is your turn to deal with a medical crisis. You may not know this, but when one is a minister, you are pretty much in people's lives from birth to death, and all of life's issues in between these two events. This means we are often called upon to visit the sick and pray for healing, and I have had this humbling experience on numerous occasions. I would often walk into a room fully prayed up and ready to share a word to someone who just received some exceedingly difficult news about their health or the health of a loved one. Yes, I quoted scriptures and emphasized that they needed to trust in God like so many other biblical characters we know from the Bible stories. After I had seemingly dispensed some comfort, I would leave that location

knowing that I had done my job and the rest was in the hand of the Lord. Please do not get me wrong; it was scary walking into a room where people are looking at you for strength and for words to help them through probably one of the scariest times of their life. Let me tell you, while I thought I understood, I was absolutely clueless until it was my turn for someone to come to me and tell me my situation was going to be all right. I will start with this first: men, your health is so important, so man up and get your butt to the doctor.

Several years ago, the doctor told me that my prostate-specific antigen (PSA) numbers were elevated, and he wanted to run more tests, which of course they did, and those tests caused more concerns after which they informed me that they wanted to do a biopsy. I was gripped with fear and panic. I could not remember all the verses that I quoted over the years. I could not remember all the encouraging words I had spoken during others' time of need. No, my friend, all I could think of was the C Word, cancer. Was I going be diagnosed with cancer and given a few months or weeks to say goodbye to all the people I loved and cared for? I went for the tests but I could not get the results that day. In fact, it was going to take several days, which seemed like an eternity to me.

As the days went by, my mind raced and raced. I could not sleep and had problems concentrating until I reached a point in which I asked God to give me peace until the results were known and to give me courage to live with whatever my diagnosis would be. I must tell you, God did just that. I completely forgot about the pending results and began to do life as I always had. In fact, Brenda and I were headed to our company's annual celebration in Washington, DC when the phone rang. I picked the call up on the car speakers. The caller informed me that he was my doctor and he wanted to discuss my PSA results. Those words fell in my lap like three tons of brick, but in the end, he stated there was no cancer and that I just had to continue with my annual regular checkup. Yes, we praised God in the car just before we parked to head upstairs, where our staff was waiting for us to start the program. We made no mention of the news because it was a time of celebration not just for me but for all the people who worked so hard to make our company successful. So do not panic; God's got it.

Reverend G's Lesson for You: *It is okay to be scared, just remember to trust God even in your darkest moment.*

Time to do Something Different?

Most of us of do not like change. It is especially difficult to change when the current circumstances are not causing you pain or costing you money. Which begs the question: why change at all? Allow me to share with you my lesson regarding knowing when it is time to change and do something different. First, I am no stranger to changing jobs because I have done that so many times, I cannot remember them all. No, the change that I am referring to in life is the path of Christianity or one's position within a religious denomination. I mention these as an example, but I believe this lesson could apply to a host of other life events. I have been in the Baptist community for what seems like forever. But I began to notice over time I did not have the same fire I once had for serving the people and serving God. I knew I needed to do something different, and I wanted to do something different. However, I just did not have the courage and probably the strength to stretch out on my faith and seek a different path of worship, a different culture of worship, and frankly just a new way of looking at how God uses different people in his work. How was I ever going to leave the black church experience and attend a place that did not reflect the culture of the black church? Wait, before you close this book and write me off, at least hear me out. What I mean is this: we have always talked about how Sunday is the most segregated day in America, but if we never do anything different, how will that ever change? It will not. To be frank, I did not set out on this path under my own sail, but it was God-planned and orchestrated. It started when we sold our home in Fairfax Station, Virginia, and decided to relocate to another state. We did all of the research on the area, to include crime rate, restaurants, entertainment, etc. However, what we did not do until after we signed the contract on our new home was look for a church. I did not specifically look for a black church; I simply looked for a place of worship. As I did my research it was only then that I recognized that black churches were limited in the area into which we were moving. It was then that the lesson sank in that I should not be looking for a church based on the color of the skin but by the character of its worship, and that is exactly what we did.

I mean think about it: when we get to heaven there will be no black churches, there will be no white churches. No, my friends, we are all equal and the same in the eyes of God. With this lesson fresh in my mind, I set out to visit churches that were in close proximity to where we lived. These visits resulted in some very touching and amazing worship experiences. It has opened not only my eyes but my mind to how God uses his people no matter the color.

Reverend G's Lesson for You: *Worship is worship, we should not care if they look like us or not.*

I Just Want to be a Good Dad

Struggles as a Newly Minted Father

Up to this point I have mentioned a lot about my stepfather and nothing at all about my biological father. Well, as I have said, I knew little about my biological father because he and my mom separated when I was a child. He did not have an active role in my life. The sad tragedy of this is that he only lived ten miles away, but he took no interest in being engaged in my life as a father. As I grew older, I would often see him walking the street or hanging out at the local clubs. He was friendly enough and spoke when he did see me, but we never had a connection that led to any meaningful communication. By all accounts he was a hard worker at the sawmill, and in my longing to connect with him, I would try and visit him on the job site just to see if he cared about me. In short, I think he cared in the best way he could but not in the manner that a little boy my age needed. The question is, why am I pointing out these facts about my relationship with my father? Well, the answer lies ahead.

When you are neglected by your father and abused by your stepfather, it is virtually impossible to comprehend that one day you will be a father and what that will look like. I was thrilled and horrified all at the same time when we discovered we were pregnant with our first child. I had no idea what to do. However, I committed to doing the opposite of what I had experienced in my life. I figured if I at least eliminated the absent father and the abusive nature of my stepfather, I would be on my way to being a good father; and that is exactly what I started doing. I remembered all the things I wanted to experience as a child and never had the opportunity, so I started doing those things with my son. Our son was born overseas while we were stationed in Germany. I can still remember the day as though it were yesterday. He entered this world in Nurnberg, Germany crying, kicking, and full of life. It was one of the proudest moments of my life. The time for second guessing whether or not I was ready for fatherhood was over. He had made his appearance, and it was time to start fulfilling my role as a father.

> **Reverend G's Lesson for You:** *Fatherhood is the greatest role a man could have in life. But let me assure you there will be challenges, there will be mistakes; but when you man up, admit when you are wrong and show love, this is how your children become strong. In the end you will know that you did the best you could as a father aka Pops.*

From Father to Grandfather

There are lots of great joys in life, like marrying the love of your life, landing the dream job, buying your first car, or having your first child. These are all life-changing events, but those joys are taken to a new level when your first grandchild arrives. Life takes on a whole new meaning about the journey ahead. My transition from fatherhood into the kingdom of grandfather came to me in my mid-40s, and man, am I loving it. You hear the cliché about it being a time for parents to get even with their kids. Well, that is not my story. I want you to know, other than slipping them some candy, BG and I try to respect and enforce the same rules that their parents employ in their home–maybe not in a full-time forceful manner but certainly keeping them on the path that their parents have them on. But nonetheless, grandkids bring a joy that makes you feel like a kid again. I mean you can play with toys, go to the zoo, eat candy, and all under the pretenses that it is for the grandkids while it really is for you. Having grandkids gives you the opportunity to tell them stories about life and what they can expect, without having to deal with all the disciplinary activities. While I draft this book, I have three amazing grandkids and a fourth one on the way. To my grandkids who all call me Papa: Matthew, Brooklynn, Logyn, and the little one the way, I am proud to be your Papa. I love my new role, and I have a great relationship with my grandchildren, and I pray that you do as well.

> **Reverend G's Lesson for You:** *Grandparents can be like Nike, just saying yes to everything.*

Reverend G's Life's Lessons Along the Way

The following lessons are from sermons I have preached over the course of many years. At the time I first preached these sermons I had no idea I would be converting many of them into a book to share with the world. I am sharing them with you because during those years an abundance of individuals have informed me how they were not only touched by the sermons but also encouraged by what was preached. So likewise, I hope that you are touched and encouraged by these lessons and that you will share them with people you love and care about.

RGWOE Lesson 1 - A Better Life

Hebrews 11:39-40 - These were all commended for their faith, yet none of them received what had been promised, since God had planned something better for us so that only together with us would they be made perfect.

Growing up, me and my best friend Mike used to watch this television series called *The Six Million Dollar Man*[1]. As part of the introduction, they would say, "We can rebuild him. We have the technology. We can make him better than he was. Better, stronger, faster." After watching the show, Mike and I would often go outside to see if we were actually stronger or faster. To our amazement, we were not stronger or faster, only tired. Then there was another TV show's theme song that stated, *"Well, we're moving on up, to the east side"*[2] *to a deluxe apartment in the sky. Moving on up, to the east side. We finally got a piece of the pie."*

This leads me to ask the question, what do these TV shows have in common? I believe the answer is this: we all desire a better life. This does not mean your life is bad or has to be bad, it just means you desire something more. Let us face the facts. We all are to some degree looking for and wanting a better life. I mean,

---
[1] https://www.nbc.com/the-six-million-dollar-man, November 7, 2021.
[2] https://www.imdb.com/title/tt0072519/, November 7, 2021.

why work hard, drive long distances, put up with bosses who just do not get you? We want our kids to have a better life than we did. The traditional marriage vows used to say for better or for worse. On its surface there is nothing wrong with working hard to achieve the level of success you believe God wants you to enjoy. But isn't life more than just things? And if you will stay with me for a few minutes, I can bring that point home. Life sometimes means going through difficult stuff. I would like for you to remember that in order for things to get better you may have to go along some rough roads. Better does not come easy, it requires sacrifice. It means you must see the big picture, it means we have to stay focused on the end result. It is like athletes seeking a position on the team, they have to better themselves and put some sweat equity into the dream.

In order to successfully navigate the challenges of life, we have to trust in God, and trust requires faith to persevere. I have come to learn that as believers we are not exempt from the troubles of life. Sometimes it seems as though there is no rope to hold on to, and the tunnel has collapsed, and the old adage of Murphy's law seems to be the flavor of the day in your life. So, the question is, what will sustain us through the tumultuous waters? I believe it is our faith in God. Allow me to unpack this a little more.

The author of Hebrews shares some insight into his thinking on the topic of faith. What we discover in chapter 11 is that the great heroes of the faith were saved and lived by faith. Faith here is not just a matter of belief, but a matter of behavior (based upon belief). The word *faith* appears twenty-four times in Hebrews chapter eleven, and the expression, *by faith*, is found nineteen times in this chapter. These heroes endured much and thus achieved much. While our struggle may not be at the immense level of these saints, they are still challenges that you and I have to sometimes overcome on a recurring basis. But even when life is good and you are at your sweet spot, there is something better ahead. Faith does not necessarily take you around the storm but sustains you right in the midst of the storm. Faith helps you climb the mountain, make it to the top, look over and say, *yep, there is another mountain ahead of me, but God has got this.*

I do not know about you, but my life is so much better because of my faith. Do not get me wrong. I have experienced my moments of doubt in the plan that God has before me. But with faith I have learned to persevere—to hold to the fact that if I can step out on faith, He is right there to catch me if or when I fall. Do you want a better life? Well, in my opinion it starts with putting your faith in Jesus. Think about this for a second, we put our faith in a lot of things that we know little or nothing about. I have never met the person who engineered the roller coaster, but I put my faith in the cart and rail that I will return safely.

Your name in the faith hall of fame. By faith, you loved people when they despitefully used you. By faith, you have endured numerous trips to the doctor. By faith, you felt like a nobody, but have seen what God has done in your life. By faith, you are giving your time and resources to spread the Word of God around the world. By faith, you have made a career switch and you did not lose pay or benefits. By faith, you know you were not supposed to get accepted into that college, but God worked it out.

My friends, lest I leave you thinking a better life means a bigger house or a higher paying job, no, these things do not even come close to the better that I am referring to. I am referring to where you will spend eternity. Why is it better? Heaven is a place of "no mores." There will be no more tears, no more pain, and no more sorrow (Revelation 21:4). There will be no more separation because death will be conquered (Revelation 20:6). The best thing about heaven is the presence of our Lord and Savior (1 John 3:2). We will be face to face with the Lamb of God who loved us and sacrificed Himself so that we can enjoy His presence in heaven for eternity.

> **RGWOE - What is the Point?** *If you want a better life, then be better at giving, loving, and sharing. Do not blame others for not doing better because truth be told, we all can do better.*

RGWOE Lesson 2 - In Between a Wall and a Crisis

2 Kings 20:1-2 In those days was Hezekiah sick unto death. And the prophet Isaiah the son of Amoz came to him, and said unto him, thus saith the Lord, Set thine house in order; for thou shalt die, and not live. 2 Then he turned his face to the wall, and prayed unto the Lord, saying…

I would like to know where you are on this lesson by asking you two questions: If you have ever been in crisis, can you say amen? If God has ever delivered you from a crisis, can you say hallelujah?"

Crisis: we all face a crisis at some point in our lives. More than likely, you have been in a crisis or maybe even right now you may be in the midst of a crisis. I would dare say that all our crises are different. In other words, my crisis may not be a crisis for you but nonetheless it poses a crisis for me. That being said, I am reminded of a time when our son was about four years old, and I received a frantic call from Brenda. This

call occurred long before cell phone with video capabilities. Brenda said, "Hon, you have to come home right now; Jeffery was playing around the glass coffee table, and the table broke, and Jeffery has broken glass in his hand and is bleeding really bad." Of course, I did what any father would do, I bolted out of the office, jumped in my car, sped home, and sprinted upstairs to our apartment. When I opened the door, there to greet me was Jeffery and he said, "Look, Daddy, I have a boo boo." I looked down and there was this little sliver of glass in his pinky finger. From this crisis event, we all had three different perspectives. My wife saw it as a crisis, my son saw it as a trophy moment, and I saw it as "how the heck am I going to explain this to my employer?" So, you can see in this small example that all of us may have a different response to a perceived or actual crisis. However, I am going to go out on a limb and say that if God sends you a message that states you shall die and not recover, all of us would perceive this as a crisis of an unprecedented nature. It does not matter the color of your skin or your age – I believe that this qualifies as a crisis from everyone's perspective. Can I get one amen?

So, in the interest of time, I want to provide you with a quick summary of how we ended up here in the twentieth chapter. In the preceding chapter, you will find that Hezekiah was at war with certain forces in the area, and that he was concerned about the Assyrian forces entering Jerusalem, so he called for the prophet Isaiah. Isaiah gave him a word from the Lord and that word was that God would not allow the Assyrian forces to enter Jerusalem.

Hezekiah's Crisis. This is where we find the story in 2 Kings Chapter 20. Let us unpack this Old Testament story and see how it is still applicable to us today. The text states that Hezekiah was sick and at the point of death. There is a difference between being sick and being at the point of death. Hezekiah was at a crisis in his life; however, the crisis was elevated to another level when he received a visit from the prophet Isaiah who told him to get his house in order, for he would die and not recover. I do not mean to minimize any issues that we go through in life, but when one receives a message like the one Hezekiah received, having a bad boss, a boring job, and long commute are no longer important. A delayed flight or rude service professional no longer registers on my radar of concern. I submit to you that this is a crisis of an unprecedented nature.

After receiving the message, let us examine how Hezekiah responded, but before I proceed with what he does, can I pause here and talk about a few things that Hezekiah did not do. Notice, he did not get upset with the messenger. He did not ask the question you or I may ask, "Why me, Lord?" No, this king turned

his head to the wall. In examining this text, I wanted to know why Hezekiah turned to the wall because the text does not provide any additional information on the king's actions. However, in some of my research it indicated that he wanted to be transparent in how he responded and did not necessarily want others to see his face. I certainly understand from a man's perspective who wants to keep the bravado edge and not let the people see that he is in trouble. However, what he does next deserves our attention.

Hezekiah's Two-step Process to Crisis Management

- **Step 1 – He prayed**
  - ◦ I've walked before you in faithfulness and with a whole heart.
  - ◦ Done what is good in your sight.
- **Step 2 – He Wept Bitterly**

In other words, Hezekiah was expressing his integrity and faithfulness and asking for healing and a longer life. Sometimes a crisis will bring tears to your eyes. Have you ever had to cry your way through a crisis? But here is where the story takes an immediate and interesting turn. Before Isaiah had left and made it to the middle court, God sent him an updated message for Hezekiah. In my humble opinion, this could be the Old Testament story where your grandmother and my grandmother coined the statement, "He may not come when you want him, but he is always on time." I know it is hard to wait on an answer from God, but when we do what is right and live faithful to His word, our situation can change. For God tells Isaiah to relay a message to Hezekiah: "I have heard your prayer and I have seen your tears."

Remember back in the second verse Hezekiah does not ask for anything? He just told God about what he had done and then he wept bitterly. But we see here in this verse that God says, "I will heal your body and defend this city." Not only was he going to receive healing, but God was adding fifteen years to his life. God was going to defend the city. That is called getting more than you ask for. You catch that when we are sincere in prayer and pour our hearts out before God, he will often give us more than we could ask for.

Hezekiah was not the only one who had gone through a crisis. I submit to you that Joseph was in crisis when his brothers sold him into slavery. John the Baptist was in a crisis when pharaoh's daughter demanded his head on a platter. When you find yourself in between a wall and a crisis, how will you respond? Will

you blame the messenger, or will you ask God *why me?* Or will you turn to the wall, and say, "Lord, please, remember that I tried to live a life that was pleasing to you. I have tried to do the right thing, and God, I am sorry for every area in which I have fallen short."

> **RGWOE - What is the Point?** *You can manage the crisis, or you can allow the crisis to manage you. The choice is yours, choose wisely. You can also blame others for the crisis but in the end, you still have to do something, so get on with it.*

RGWOE Lesson 3 - Thirsty for More than Water

Exodus 17:1-2 *"The whole Israelite community set out from the Wilderness of Sin, traveling from place to place as the Lord commanded. They camped at Rephidim, but there was no water for the people to drink. 2 So they quarreled with Moses and said, "Give us water to drink."*

About seventy-one percent of the Earth's surface is covered in water, and the oceans hold about ninety-six percent of all Earth's water. Water also exists in the air as water vapor, in rivers and lakes, in icecaps and glaciers, in the ground as soil moisture and in aquifers, and even in you and your dog. Americans spend more than eleven billion dollars on bottled water per year. Recently I was at a church and learned just how important water is when they sponsored "World Vision Water" for those in need, who had to walk six kilometers just to reach drinking water. So, it should be easy to understand just how important water is in our lives. But the question I want you to think about today is: have you ever been so thirsty that the only thing that could quench your thirst was a cold glass of water?

When reading the first verse in this chapter, one immediately takes a pause at the statement "Wilderness of sin." Please note this does not mean they were living in the wilderness of sin as commonly known as the sin of disobedience. No, there was an actual place on the map called Wilderness of Sin. If I could side bar for a moment, can you imagine if you were from the Wilderness of Sin and you were applying for a position at the church, and they ask you where you live and you said, "I have lived in the Wilderness of Sin for all of my adult life." Or if someone asked you where you are going for vacation and you replied, "I am packing the family up in the minivan and we are all headed to the Wilderness of Sin." I could go on, but I am sure you get my idea.

I think we have to understand the nature of the situation. Have you ever been at the point in which you were so thirsty, all you wanted was a drink of water? It is like a Coke or any other flavored drink just cannot quench the thirst you feel. Well, imagine how they must have felt after making the journey from the Wilderness of Sin to Rephidim, all the while thinking, "Man, I cannot wait until we reach the front. Dude, I'm going to find me the biggest jar and sit down and have me a cool drink of water," only to find out upon their arrival that there was no water to drink. Of course, when things do not work out the way people want them to work out, somebody must take the blame. It was not so long ago that Moses led them out of Egypt; the splitting of the Red Sea no longer seemed like a recent miracle. It seemed like an event in the distant past, long ago forgotten. So, they took their frustrations out on Moses, and Moses asked them two questions: Why are you bothering me and why do you test God?

Trust me, I can relate to the Israelites because I was once in the wilderness of sin and this wilderness of sin was not a geographical spot on the map. No, sin had caused me to end up in the wilderness. And just like the Israelites I quarreled with people and argued with individuals. I had to blame others for where I had arrived in my life. I was tired and was thirsting for more than just water. Because Dasani could not quench my thirst, and Aquafina brought me no satisfaction. Only a spiritual connection to Christ would suffice. Because I found myself with no peace and no direction. I said to someone, "If you had not treated me the way you treated me, I would not have been here." I had it better when I was doing what I wanted to do—when I was a non-believer of the Bible. But it brought me no peace and I found myself thirsting for more than my selfish desires. But then I became a Christian and verses like, "Blessed are those who hunger and thirst for righteousness, for they shall be satisfied," gave me a whole new perspective on life.

> **RGWOE - What is the Point?** *If we want more out of life then we need to do more in life. What are you thirsting for today? More importantly, what will you do to quench that thirst? May I suggest you drink of the living water which is Jesus Christ?*

RGWOE Lesson 4 - Courage in the Face of Adversity

Joshua 1 :6-7 "*Be strong and courageous, because you will lead these people to inherit the land I swore to their ancestors to give them. Be strong and very courageous. Be careful to obey all the law my servant Moses gave you; do not turn from it to the right or to the left, that you may be successful wherever you go.*"

In preparing for this lesson, I am reminded of a time when my son was in high school, and I received a call from my son's guidance counselor. The counselor informed me that Jeffery had gotten into a fight with another student and that I needed to get home with all due haste. Of course, I headed home like a rocket taking off from its launching pad. As I was driving home, a thousand thoughts ran through my mind on how I was going to punish him, oops, I mean discipline him for this unacceptable behavior. And just as I was in line of sight to glimpse him at the bus stop and my blood pressure was shooting off the charts, my phone rang, and it was again the guidance counselor. The counselor told me, "Mr. Gaines, I am so sorry, but your son did not start the fight, he was actually trying to stop the fight between his classmates. In other words, my son was demonstrating courage in the face of adversity. Which leads me into today's lesson: *Courage in the Face Adversity.*

So here in Joshua chapter one, we now see there is a change in leadership, and I think it is important to not rush past a key identifier in verse one. For the text states that Joshua was Moses' assistant. To fully understand the challenge that is set before Joshua, I think it is important to spotlight some of the significant things about the person he was replacing. Moses was a legend in his time, and even today in Christian culture he is legendary. He had seen the burning bush; demanded that Pharaoh let God's people go; Moses had escaped Pharaoh's army, crossed the Red Sea, delivered the Ten Commandments… I could go on, but you get the idea.

Joshua was one of two spies who returned with an encouraging report from the land of Canaan. Therefore, Joshua eventually goes from being an assistant to the man in charge. Not just the man in charge but the man that comes after Moses. Those were some big shoes to fill. What a promotion, what a change in life station. It is one thing to replace someone, but it is a whole other issue to replace someone like Moses. He had led the Israelites for forty years; to put that in perspective, it is ten U.S. presidential terms, ten election cycles. Filling in or following someone who had overcome so much could be a daunting task.

Sometimes when I am accepting a new position or role, I try to find out about the person that had the job before me, so I make inquiries. When I hear that everyone in the office showed up for the person's departure and there was not a dry eye after that person gave their farewell address, I immediately know that I have my work cut out for me. However, on the other hand if during the inquiry I hear that no one showed up for their departure and the party started after that person walked out the door, then I have a different approach. God appoints Joshua to the government in the stead of Moses, gives him an ample commission, full instructions, and great encouragement.

A Time of Change - So, today's lesson finds us at a time of change. We find Joshua with a promotion and dealing with grief, not to mention all of the people that Joshua found himself in charge of. Change can and does bring on uncertainty. When many of us see the new year we see it as opportunity for change, something new or a different direction. But no doubt there will be challenges in the new year. However, the quintessential question is: how will you and I face the change and the challenges it brings? I believe that it will take courage to overcome any adversity. With change comes challenges. Maybe you have experienced a life change from single to married or married to single or maybe you are a new parent. Maybe you have lost the love of your life and you find yourself faced with all kinds of challenges. I want to encourage you to have courage in the face of adversity.

Maybe this past year may have thrown you a few curve balls, unexpected turbulence, unanticipated expenses that not only set the budget back but blew away all your savings. And you are thinking you have faced so many adversities in the past year that maybe the load will be lighter in the new year because nobody likes adversity. Adversity, we would all like to avoid it, but the reality of life is that adversity is simply unavoidable. In fact, I would make the leap in saying adversity helps define who we truly are as people and as Christians. If we are honest, if there were two doors in life and one said *Adverse-Free Living* and the other said *Adversity in Abundance, come on in*, which door would you choose to walk through? My friend do not allow adversity to change or hinder the plan that God has for you. Because we all need to be reminded that no human shall be able to stand in the way of God's plan for our lives. I do not care how they try, what they say, what strings they pull to try and undermine the plan that God has for you, they will fail. Oh yes, it may certainly be unpleasant, and it may even cost you grief and pain. But courage will take you through it. Heroes do not become heroes by running away from the fight; no, heroes stay in the fight. David does not sprint from Goliath. Daniel does not hide from the lions. Paul is not taking a scenic tour of the prison. No, these individuals had courage in the midst of adversity and so can you and me.

"I was with Moses" - God was reminding Joshua that he was with Moses, and obviously Joshua had witnessed the many miracles that God had performed under Moses' leadership. Then he was aware of the things that God could do for His people. For God says, "Do not turn from it to the right hand or to the left." In this ever-changing world one can easily be distracted by things that are going on around us. But the author reminds us to stay focused.

When I was in the military and the drill sergeants were teaching us to march, one of the things that was drilled into you day in and day out is, "Do not look around you and be distracted. Trust that the person next to you is doing their job. It is called 'eyes straight forward.'" In a sense, Joshua reminds us to not look around but to trust that God is doing what he is supposed to do. Stay the course with eyes straight forward. I am reminding you as we prepare to enter change to stay the course; do not get distracted by what the enemy throws our way.

Depart from a reckless mouth. Guard what you say. The Bible says that life and death are in the power of the tongue. Choose your words carefully for they speak volumes about what you believe and think. It is important to meditate on the Bible, day and night. It is hard for other things to crowd your mind when you begin to meditate on the Word of God. Since adversity does not take vacations or sick days, we must continually meditate on the Word of God. Do an inventory of the apps that are on your smart phone. If at the end of the inventory there are no Bible apps, I submit to you that maybe it is time to open the app store and download one. These apps will assist you in meditating day and night on the Word of God.

"God will not leave you or forsake you" (Hebrews 13:5). It has been said that friends will betray you and family may walk out on you, but Jesus will never leave you. Please know that in every event with all your issues, your little quirks and your mood swings and attitude adjustments, Jesus will not leave you. He is there with you no matter how dark the day or rough the road. God is with you, my friend.

The Lord Your God is with You Wherever You Go – It is reassuring knowing that no matter where we go God is with us. You can catch Uber to the airport, jump on a flight that will last sixteen hours, transfer to boat and travel the oceans, yet our God is still there with you. He is there in the emergency room. He is there with you in the board meeting. He is there with you in the big office or the little cubicle. If you are serving in Afghanistan or Pakistan, God is with you. He is there with your children on the school bus and on the playground. God is there, with the police officer or EMT, our God is still protecting you.

Good Success Wherever You Go - Be Strong and Courageous. Looking back over my life I remember that what God has done for others He will do for me. I am reminded of those who had courage in the face of adversity, for it took courage for Queen Esther to say, "If I perish let me perish, I am going to see the king." It was courage when Job uttered the words, "Though he slays me, yet will I trust in him." So, as we approach this new year, I am reminded that it is not the finish line, ending our work. We still have work to do, and just as the Israelites crossed the river Jordan, when we cross over into next year, God is still with us. For he said He would never leave us or forsake us. So, we have endured some bumps and bruises in this past year. But be of good courage, knowing that God has your back. It may get dark, but the sun will shine again. And as you walk with the Lord, do not veer to the left or to the right but keep your eyes toward heaven and your mind stayed on God. And when you encounter adverse situations, I want you to meditate on His word day and night.

> **RGWOE - What is the Point?** *"We find courage to stand when we kneel before the Lord."*

RGWOE Lesson 5 - Do Not Let Life Pin You to the Wall.

1 Samuel 18:10-11 The next day an evil spirit from God came forcefully on Saul. He was prophesying in his house, while David was playing the lyre, as he usually did. Saul had a spear in his hand, and he hurled it, saying to himself, "I will pin David to the wall." But David eluded him twice.

Some years ago, while stationed at Fort Huachuca, Arizona, I found myself being rushed to the emergency room. Upon arrival I was in so much pain that they rolled me into the emergency room and began running tests, but after all the testing was complete the doctors could not determine the cause of my pain. The doctors gave me various kinds of medications to take, and those medications did not work. As I lay there phasing in and out of consciousness, I remember my pastor at that time seated in the corner of my room with his Bible. When I saw him, I knew at once that I was in trouble and the fight of my life. Though the pain seemed like it went on for an eternity, I ended up in that ER for almost a week. My pastor prayed, the church prayed, and of course my wife was constantly praying. Eventually, the pain eased, and I was released and sent home

with no pain and with no real diagnosis of what happened to me. It is in times like these when you have been victorious in a fight that you just want to take a breather and not worry or wonder about the next fight. It is with this as a backdrop that I present today's lesson: *Do Not Let Life Pin You to the Wall.*

You see, many of us can quote the David and Goliath story. It was the fight of a lifetime; I mean it is legendary: boy slays giant. But let us consider what happened to David after this magnificent victory. The story unfolds with David and the king returning home, no doubt from a difficult day of fighting the Philistines. You know how it is when you have had a hard day's work and you have nailed that assignment, did a killer presentation, I mean, you were in the zone. You were riding the preferable cloud nine analogy. Your achievement actually became public. As you were enjoying this moment, women from various cities wanted to express their gratitude and decided to come and praise you instead of your jealous employer. This is what happened to the returning soldiers, including young David. Please note that they went out to meet Saul who was king at the time, but their singing struck a nerve in Saul when they ended up giving the king's servant the higher praise. For they said Saul struck down thousands but David ten thousands. So, while others are singing your praise, someone is plotting your demise. Please remember that life after the fight still has its challenge. Be careful! Everyone who shows up for your promotion party is not happy you were promoted. Saul eyed David from that day on. He went to bed that night stewing in his anger; he tossed and turned, walked the palace halls restless about a song that David did not compose or sing, a song that David had no knowledge of. From David's perspective, he was doing what a loyal soldier does. Then it was not exceptionally long before a bitter and harmful spirit entered Saul. Life can change at the blink of eye and when you least expect it.

However, on the other side of this story, David was chilling playing some smooth jazz music for Saul on his harp. Then in one fatal second, the king grabbed a spear and hurled it at David. It was not long before that the king was singing David's praise for slaying the giant. It was not so long ago that the king so admired this man that he refused to let him return home. But life can change on you instantly, and often when you least expect it. When you are in a moment of celebration, the enemy is eyeing you and sizing you up, trying to determine the best time to strike you down. Life is not always easy. It can be filled with difficulties, regrets, and disappointments, and will often try and pin you to the wall. The text states that Saul was afraid because God was with David. So do not be afraid, my friend, God is with us.

When the demotion becomes a promotion - So, Saul removed him and gave him command of a thousand. Since Saul could not kill David, he decided he would remove him and demote him down to being in charge of a thousand men. But I am reminded that when one door is closed God can open a better door. So, while Saul thought he could pin David against a wall by removing him and putting him in charge of a smaller force, God had other plans. For the text states, "But David had success in all his undertaking for God was with him."

> **RGWOE - What is the Point?** *Sometimes when you are shining, others will try and dull the shine that God has on your life. Do not let that happen, keep on shining.*

RGWOE Lesson 6 - Paid in Full

Matthew 18:26-27 *At this the servant fell on his knees before him. 'Be patient with me,' he begged, 'and I will pay back everything.' The servant's master took pity on him, canceled the debt, and let him go.*

Several years ago, our daughter accepted a new job, so she informed Brenda and me that she was going to take us out for brunch to celebrate our wedding anniversary, her treat. To be clear, when you tell me free and food in the same sentence, I am in. When Candice informed me of this occasion, in my mind I was thinking we would go to Bob Evans or have some of those wonderful blueberry pancakes from Cracker Barrel. But she informed us that she had made reservations for brunch at the Four Seasons in Georgetown, Washington DC. I was thinking, *"Dang, how big is her pay increase?"* I am here to tell you that when we arrived at the Four Seasons, they had everything laid out; shrimp, steaks, fresh fruit, cook to order omelets, and Belgian waffles. It was one those proud parent moments for Brenda and me. Then the server brought that little portfolio over that contained the bill and I could see the look of joy and pleasure that Candice had on her face; she was picking up the tab for her parents. She grabbed the portfolio with eagerness and opened it, and that is when the gap of what you thought it would cost intersected with the actual cost. We immediately saw the smile drop from her face, and we could see tears welling up in her eyes. So, I grabbed the bill, and immediately, the smile on my face disappeared and tears welled in my eyes as well. After we gasped at the price, Brenda and I told her we would cover the cost. She insisted that she would pay the bill in full but noted that this brunch also covered Mother's Day, Father's Day, birthdays, and Christmas gifts. She took the check and paid it in full. Which leads me to today's topic: *Paid in Full*

In this parable, the king decides that it is time to settle accounts, and he calls this man forward to demand payment on all accounts. After the king hears how much money the man owes, he immediately forgives him of all the debt. Can you imagine if all the organizations that you owed called you tomorrow and stated that all of your accounts are paid in full today: the mortgage company, the car loan, the credit card, and let us not forget the coveted student loans. What would be your reaction? I am sure it would be similar to this man that was standing before the king.

This man owed the king ten thousand talents, which was a huge sum of money. To put this in perspective, my research indicates a talent was a monetary unit worth about twenty years' wages for a laborer. So, if you do the math, it will take one person 200,000 years to pay off this debt. So, in order to settle the debt, the king ordered him to be sold along with his wife and children, plus their belongings. The king was going to sell all of this guy's belongings: the house on the cul-de-sac, the Lexus, and flat screen TV with the nice Apple watch, along with the man's family.

The servant, knowing that he had gotten himself into a mess that he could not get himself out of, fell on his knees and began to sing that old familiar song by Albertine Walker, "Please Be Patient with Me."[3] Here is the extraordinary part of the story: the king not only released him but forgave him of the debt. In essence his account was "paid in full." Now I do not know about you, but in my mind, it would have been praising-God-time in the Gaines' household. I would not have cared who was watching or what they said, can I get my praise on?

But, no, the story takes a turn, and if you do not have previous knowledge of this story, you simply do not see the twist coming. This same servant went out looking for someone who owed him some money and he found someone that was indebted to him for a hundred denarii[4]. The denarius was one day's wage for a typical day laborer, who worked six days a week with a Sabbath day of rest. This man laid hands on him and started choking him, demanding that he pay his debt. But his fellow servant pleaded the familiar words that were spoken by a choked, hoarse voice, "Please have patience with me." But the man refused and sent his fellow servant to prison. The unforgiving servant had developed a critical case of blessing amnesia; forgetting that he was once shown mercy. But notice that others are watching you, and they see and have heard how you

---

[3] https://www.flashlyrics.com/lyrics/albertina-walker/please-be-patient-with-me-46 November 9, 2021.
[4] https://www.collinsdictionary.com/us/dictionary/english/denarii January 27, 2022.

received your blessing but also how unfairly this servant was toward his fellow servant who owed so much less compared to what he owed the king: 10K talents vs 100 denarii. Word went back to the king who promptly put his butt in jail until the debt could be paid in full.

Conclusion - This passage has several distinct aspects. I could have addressed money management. I could have addressed the treatment of others. I could have focused on being patient with one another. While all of these are good points to make, I particularly want to focus on giving and receiving forgiveness. I submit to you that while you and I were in our sins, we owed a debt that we could not pay. Isaiah 53 is for you. Can you feel the weight of these words? Do you sense the wonder of what Jesus has done for you? *"Surely, he has borne our griefs and carried our sorrows; yet we esteemed him stricken, smitten by God, and afflicted. But he was pierced for our transgressions; he was crushed for our iniquities; upon him was the chastisement that brought us peace, and with his wounds we are healed. All we like sheep have gone astray; we have turned—everyone—to his own way; and the Lord has laid on him the iniquity of us all. He was oppressed, and he was afflicted, yet he opened not his mouth; like a lamb that is led to the slaughter, and like a sheep that before its shearers is silent, so he opened not his mouth.*

But Jesus paid it all, and all to Him we owe. When they were beating Jesus, I can say there was payment made toward our account. When they pounded the nails in Jesus' hands and feet, there was a payment made on our account. When they hung Jesus on the cross, that was a payment made on our account. When they laid Jesus in the tomb, that was payment made on our account. But early Sunday morning, when Jesus arose from the tomb, our account owed was paid in full. And I do not know about you, but I am doing a little bit of what the unforgiving servant did. I am going to find someone that has a debt, but I am not going to tell them to pay me. I am going to remind them that Jesus paid it all and all to him I owe. So, if you find yourself in a place you do not want to be, fall on your knees, and ask God to forgive you of your debt of sin.

> **RGWOE - What is the Point?** *Forgiveness should be like a baton in a relay team in the Olympics. Please pass the baton on to the next person and the next person.*

RGWOE Lesson 7 - Moving from Complaining to Praise

Habakkuk 3:17–19 *Though the fig tree does not bud and there are no grapes on the vines, though the olive crop fails, and the fields produce no food, though there are no sheep in the pen and no cattle in the stalls, yet I will rejoice in the LORD, I WILL BE JOYFUL IN GOD MY SAVIOR. The Sovereign LORD IS MY STRENGTH; HE MAKES MY FEET LIKE THE FEET OF A DEER, HE ENABLES ME TO TREAD ON THE HEIGHTS.*

As a child, I grew up living next door to my future wife's grandfather. Her grandfather was a kind and gentle man. In fact, such a kind man that he gave me my first job around the age of nine. He was the sort of man that everyone liked to be around and talk with. In fact, on many occasions, while on the way back home from work should have taken twenty minutes, it often took hours because he would stop by houses on the way home, pull up by the front porch, never get out of the car but just caringly talk with people. For some reason he took a liking to me, and one day after work when we were headed home, he stopped by the hamburger place and asked me what I wanted. I told him that I wanted a hamburger and he asked how many. I told him I wanted one and he asked, "Are you sure?" I responded yes, and he said, "I am going to order you four." What I did not know at the time was that he was treating me to a place call Krystal's which offered small burgers similar to White Castle. And of course, I devoured all four of them. He was just that type of grandfather figure to me in my early life, just a kind and gentle man. However, if you wanted to see his demeanor change, start complaining about stuff that did not matter and you would see a completely different side of him. Back in the day, neighbors did not care whose child you were, if you did something wrong, you received immediate, swift, and on-the-spot correction. And if Brenda's grandfather heard you complaining about something, he would often say, "You had better stop that complaining before I give you something to complain about."

All of Us Complain - I imagine that all of us at some point in life complain about something. If it is not the weather, it is the traffic. If not the traffic, then it is how slow the checkout line is moving at the grocery store. But I dare say that most of us move on and just sort of deal with it. But have you ever been around a person who just complains about everything all the time? You say good morning and they say, what is good about it? You say praise the Lord and they say, why? You say the pastor preached a wonderful sermon and they say, yes, but he preached too long. Which leads us to where we are in today's lesson where I will hang the tag of *Moving from Complaining to Praise*. In order to understand the importance of the verses, we need to go back to the beginning of Habakkuk.

Habakkuk lived in seventh-century Judah, probably during the latter part of King Josiah's reign and the godless reigns of the kings that followed. At the time of Habakkuk, the Assyrian Empire was nearing its end. Babylon's power was growing, and social injustice reigned in Jerusalem. It was a time of horrible spiritual decline; Habakkuk was a man greatly troubled by what was happening. He wanted to reconcile what he saw with what he believed. He saw that Judah had fallen and turned away from God. She had given herself over to false gods and evil pursuits. Habakkuk did not understand what was going on and why God was seemingly letting it happen. So, Habakkuk did what most of us do or will do, and that is have a conversation with God; and in this conversation with God, Habakkuk expressed his complaints about the situation.

Habakkuk's Complaints - "O Lord, how long shall I cry for help, and you will not hear? Or cry to you "Violence!" and you will not save? Why do you make me see iniquity, and why do you idly look at wrong? Destruction and violence are before me; strife and contention arise." (Habakkuk 1:1-3)

To understand the significance of what Habakkuk was saying in these verses, I needed to know the importance of several things Habakkuk mentions in the last verses of his prophecy: the fig tree, vines, the olive, and the herds in the stall. Habakkuk finally comes to a place of total trust in God to do the right thing in every instance; but let us see the significance of it.

First, let us examine the fig tree. The fig tree is the third tree mentioned by name in the Hebrew Bible. The first is the tree of life and the second is the tree of the knowledge of good and evil. Adam and Eve used the leaves of the fig tree to sew garments for themselves after the Fall, when they realized that they were naked (Genesis 3:7). The fig was an important food source for both humans and animals. In addition to being a food source, the bark and roots from fig trees were used for manufacturing items such as bark cloth and shields. The fig tree was important to the economy at the time, and not having the blossoms occur is similar to oranges not growing in Florida or potatoes refusing to bud in Idaho.

Now let us turn our attention to the herds in the stall. The flock of sheep, abandoned out in the field shall be cut off, either by wolf or other predators. They must be led into the fold, where they were won't to be safe. Now they were in greatest danger, and that is because they may be swept away all at once.

How do we move from complaining to praise? - I will rejoice (Habakkuk 3:18) - Makes my feet like the hind's feet: What exactly is "hind's feet?" A hind is a female deer[5] that can place her back feet exactly where her front feet stepped. Not one inch off! She is able to run with abandon! In times of danger, she is able to run securely and not get "off track." The hind is able to scale difficult terrain and elude predators.

Now can you see why the prophet talked about the hind's feet? For when we trust in God and we find ourselves on rough terrain, and the enemy is trying to run us down, Lord plant my feet like that of the deer. I will not slip, and I will not fall, for you are with me through the ups and the downs and the twists and turns. You are my very present help in the time of storm. When the predators surround me, and they think that they have me cornered, I will rejoice, for you are my strength.

In summary - He started off complaining but ended up praising. Is not life like that? Sometimes if we are not careful, we will let our eyes and mind dictate how we respond as opposed to responding with our faith in God. Oh, I am not here to pick on Habakkuk because given the same situation, I am not sure if you or I would not have come to the same conclusion. God, what is going on here? Have you ever been to the point where it just seems like things are not going to work out at all and you thought to yourself, *O Lord, how long shall I cry for help, and you will not hear me? God, I need to hear from you. I have been fasting and praying, reading your Bible, I have added your name to my prayer list, but the situation does not appear to change. God, are you not from everlasting to everlasting?*

Habakkuk was not the first one to express their complaints to God. The first complainer was Adam, who after he and Eve disobeyed, complained to God that "the woman you put here with me – she gave me some fruit from the tree, and I ate it" (Genesis 3:12). However, the book of Job offers the most in the way of complaints toward God, and yet Job did not sin. So, there is no doubt that we will all at some point in our lives complain about things. But the quintessential question is can we change our complaints into praise? If in the morning you open the refrigerator door and there is no food inside, if the car will not start, and your job is terminated; if the bank goes out of business and you cannot get the few nickels you placed there for safekeeping, how will you respond? If I lose all that I have, I am still going to rejoice. Why? For God is my strength. There is no way I can make it on my own. You see, I tried it on my own before and I found myself

---

5   https://animals.mom.com/hind-animal-2707.html November 9, 2021.

in a world of mess that my mother could not get me out of. All my friends had gone their way, the strip club could not fix it. There was only one way out, and that was to fall on my knees and say, "Lord, I need you. Help me to praise you in the midst of my storm."

One can understand how Habakkuk felt, when he saw all of the difficult things that were happening to the people of God. It was hard for him to serve an awesome and powerful God, but yet see all of the destruction before him. Maybe you and I would have arrived with the same thought process. But let us not pick on the prophet, for I dare say that some of us, if not all of us, have found ourselves in difficult circumstances or situations and we have that ole familiar question, "God, why is this happening to me? I have been serving you for an exceptionally long time. I have worked in the church, and I have given my tithes. But it seems like when I make one step forward, life kicks me back two steps. Oh God, did you hear my prayers? I mean, I cry all night long when I see what is being reported on the news. I wonder, God, are you still with me?" I wish Habakkuk could have the words of the late Reverend Paul Jones. *"I've had some good days, I've had some hills to climb, I've had some weary days, and some sleepless nights, but when I look around, and I think things over, all of my good days outweigh my bad days, I won't complain*[6].

> **RGWOE - What is the Point?** *You can choose to complain about the situation which probably will not change a thing, or you can praise God in the midst of the situation, and God can change you or the situation. I encourage you to choose wisely.*

---

[6] https://www.walmart.com/ip/I-Won-t-Complain/55682006 November 9, 2021.

RGWOE Lesson 8 - The Power of Prayer

James 5:16 - Therefore confess your sins to each other and pray for each other so that you may be healed. The prayer of a righteous person is powerful and effective.

In thinking and praying about the power of prayer I came across this simple prayer in my research. The prayer is this: "Almighty God, we acknowledge our dependence on Thee, and we beg thy blessings upon us, our parents, our teachers, and our country." This prayer promoted good moral character, provided spiritual training, and helped combat juvenile delinquency. In reading this prayer I am sure that some of you may be wondering just what is the origin of this prayer. This was the prayer that resulted in the 1962 United States Supreme Court voting 8 -1 to make the public recitation of prayer in public school unlawful.

Prayer is a weapon that the adversary has no defense against. Prayer can travel any distance, overcome any language barrier, defeat doubt, lift souls, move mountains, raise the dead, protect singleness, heal a divorcee, fix a broken marriage, and restore friendships. Prayer can get you the deluxe corner office when you are only qualified for something smaller than a cubicle.

The first thing I want to encourage you to do is pray for one another. For the verse states that we need to pray for one another. You may not be able to help me when I am in a monetary crisis. You may not be able to pick me up from the airport, and you may not be able to drop off some food for me, but there is one thing I know you can do for me and that is pray for me. For the prayers of a righteous person has great power.

The power of prayer. James then switches to what I call a case in point or what we refer to as an example of someone who had great power, and the text states that Elijah was such a person. In order to fully understand the context of why the author chose to use Elijah as an example of a righteous person exercising the power of prayer, one needs to go back to 1 Kings 17 and 18. So, for the purpose of brevity, I am going to give you the executive summary of who and what Elijah did. Elijah the Tishbite was a prophet from the settlers in Gilead. "I serve the LORD, the God of Israel," Elijah said to Ahab. "As surely as the LORD lives, no rain or dew will fall during the next few years unless I command it." I believe we have to be like Elijah. We need to speak to the situation that we serve a God that is all powerful, all-knowing, and is located everywhere.

Elijah climbed to the top of Mount Carmel, where he bent down to the ground with his head between his knees. He told the servant, "Go look toward the sea." The servant went and looked. "I don't see anything," he said. Elijah told him to go and look again. This happened seven times. But on the seventh time, the servant said, "I see a small cloud, the size of a human fist, coming from the sea." Elijah told the servant, "Go to Ahab and tell him to get his chariot ready and rush home now. Otherwise, the rain will stop him." After a brief time, the sky was covered with dark clouds. The wind began to blow, and soon a heavy rain began a flashflood. Ahab entered into his chariot and started back to Jezreel. The Lord gave his power to Elijah, who tightened his clothes around him and ran ahead of King Ahab all the way to Jezreel.

My dear friend, please remember that it was prayer that opened the Red Sea. It was prayer that raised Lazarus from the dead. It was prayer that healed the servant of the centurion. It was Jesus praying in the garden, "If this cup can pass let it pass, but not my will but God your will be done." Many of us recognize that it was the power of prayer that brought us through the stupidity of our youth, through dangers seen and unseen. It was the power of prayer which brought the birth of our children. It is the power of prayer that helped that teenage child cross the finish line at high school graduation.

Well, my friends, as I bring this lesson to a close, I want to go back to where I started—talking about removing prayer from school. So, while the Supreme Court was voting to outlaw prayer in 1962, something else was happening. It is a story about a little boy born to a poor family in a little remote obscure hospital. This child knew nothing about the law preventing prayer in school. But this little boy found himself struggling in elementary school barely knowing how to read and write, which ultimately led to his placement in special education classes; flunking class, held back a grade, and ultimately dropping out of high school without a high school diploma. Still, he knew nothing about the law preventing prayer in school, for he never really prayed himself, so why would the law mean anything to him? As a result, this boy found himself struggling through life until someone special to him reminded him about the power of prayer. So, he prayed that God would connect him with a church girl who ultimately became his wife. From there he was encouraged to go back to school and take prayer along with him. He did just that earned his GED and went on to earn several graduate-level degrees. It was during this time that he realized that while the law was passed in 1962 about school prayer, he prayed in almost all of his classes. He not only prayed for his classmates and professors, but he prayed for his colleges and universities. That, my friends, is the power of prayer. While they can take prayer out of school, they can never take school out of our prayers. And yes, I am the boy in this story, born the same year this law was passed. I know the power of prayer. For you see, I have been to my children's

school, and I have prayed. I have been to some of your children's schools, and I have prayed. I have gone to numerous colleges and prayed. As long as there are exams in school, there is prayer. As long there are SATs, there will be prayer in school.

> **RGWOE - What is the Point?** *Prayer is the most powerful tool available to you. Prayer does not change with the times and is not affected by political correctness. Prayer is the one tool that no one can ever take from you, so please do not give it away by abandoning your prayer life.*

RGWOE Lesson 9 - The Practice of Prayer

Luke 18:4-5 - *"For some time he refused. But finally he said to himself, 'Even though I don't fear God or care what people think, yet because this widow keeps bothering me, I will see that she gets justice, so that she won't eventually come and attack me!'"*

My friends, there are at least three times in life that we all need to pray, and that is before something happens, while something is happening, and after something has happened in our lives. While there are three times we need to pray, it has been my experience that most of us who pray do so the most when something difficult is happening in our lives. But if we were proactive long before something happens, it has been the experience of many that we respond differently and not as novice communicators with God. And so, it is on this day I would like to leave you with the lesson: *The Practice of Prayer*.

Interesting to note that it takes approximately 10,000 hours of practice to become a world-class musician[7]. Conversely, a minority of athletes have reached world-class status after more than 3,000 hours of "purposeful training." Olympic gymnasts require nearly 9,000 hours of practice just to qualify for the Olympics with no guarantee of winning a medal. I would dare say that in life there are very few people who can do certain things without even practicing them. Also, for the rest of us normal folks, in order to become better at something, we have to practice quite regularly.

---

[7] https://vitals.lifehacker.com/it-doesn-t-take-10-000-hours-to-become-an-olympian-1796514880

Confession time: Back when I was a private in the U.S. Army, I found myself in basic training trying to learn how to march and I just could not get it right. The drill sergeant would always say "Private Gaines, you are out of step and causing disruption to the unit," which was followed by me and the squad members doing a whole lot of pushups. Try as I might, I still could not get the marching part down until one day the drill sergeant gave orders that if I could not do certain marching moves correctly, I would go to the back of the line for dinner until I did it right. Now if you want me to pay attention to what you are saying, start messing with my food. It was without delay that I decided I was going to practice on my own and proceeded to do so. I would practice at night, on the weekends, and during the occasional lunch break. Over time I became better at marching. In fact, I would often find myself at the front of the dinner line which made me practice even more. This resulted in yours truly being selected to lead other troops in marching movements, and ultimately, I became a member of the honor guard for the unit I was assigned to. And so, with our prayer life, it requires dedication, commitment, and practice. I believe that in order to succeed in prayer you have to practice prayer.

First and foremost, these are words that Jesus himself is saying to his disciples. He tells them a parable. A parable is defined as a simple story used to illustrate a moral or spiritual lesson, as told by Jesus in the Gospels.[8] But before Jesus went into the specifics of the parable, He told us to always pray and not lose heart. You have to wonder why Jesus would tell us these two important aspects of the text before he even starts the discussion of the parable. Our savior knew what His followers would be faced with and what we would have to endure as Christians. He knew that we would be persecuted but not forsaken. He knew that we would be struck down but not destroyed. So, as I looked at the two phrases "always pray" and "don't lose heart." My first thoughts are we must "always pray." And after a careful exegetical analysis of the word 'always," I conclude that it means, continuously, never ceasing, 24/7, and at all times. Not just when an emergency shows up or you need something, but we must practice our prayer life with God every day. You see, the thing about practicing your prayers is that it becomes natural over time. It becomes easier, you look forward to praying, and if for some reason you were in a rush and forgot to pray, you will miss it and yearn to pray. Here again Jesus provides encouragement to us with these simple words, "Do not lose heart." If you are walking by sight and not by faith, it is quite easy to lose heart. When we are bombarded day in and day out by negative events and thoughts, when life has its breathtaking moments, when it seems like no one understands, do not ever, ever lose heart.

---

8 http://www.patheos.com/blogs/christiancrier/2014/05/22/what-is-a-parable-a-bible-definition/

Jesus tells this parable about a judge that did not fear God, nor did he have any respect for man. If you have not been practicing your prayer and run into someone like this judge, it will make you wish you knew how to get a prayer through to God. Let me say it in a more relevant vernacular. You see, having to deal with someone who does not respect God or you as a person will make you pray every day. Having a boss that does not fear God or respect what you do at the job will make you pray. Having a neighbor that does not respect the HOA or the fact that you live next door to them will make you pray. Having a spouse that does not respect the boundaries of your marriage or what you bring to the table will make you pray.

However, in the parable there was this widow who did not care about the fact that the judge did not respect man or care for God. All she wanted was justice against her adversary. The Bible does not state what the specifics were in her case but states that all she wanted was justice. But this judge kept on refusing to give her justice. She would not back down, she would not give up, and she would not lose heart. In fact, it sounds like the more he denied her the more steam she picked up. The judge stated she was never going to stop, so he would give her justice because she was getting on his last nerve. So, it really was not about the widow getting justice; it was about the judge getting some peace and quiet. Then Jesus says, "Hear what the unrighteous judge says, and will not God give justice to his elect, who cry to him day and night?" Practice your prayer both day and night from the rising of the sun until the going down of the same.

Will he delay long over them? Sometimes it seems like God has not heard your prayer but keep practicing your prayer and do not lose heart. The airline may not get you there on time and the metro train may not always open doors for you, but God is not delayed, for nothing can delay an all knowing and powerful God. I tell you; he will give justice to you speedily.

When I was young, we had to practice our prayer, and I still remember that prayer. It goes like this: *Now I lay me down to sleep, I pray the Lord my soul to keep. If I should die before I wake, I pray the Lord my soul to take.* But as I became older this prayer was not enough to help me break through the struggles and issues of life. I had adult-sized problems, so I needed adult-sized prayers.

It is easy to leave with a conclusion that the main point of the parable is about the widow that did not stop until she received justice. However, I submit to you that there is a much more significant takeaway, which is this: If this unrighteous judge who does not care about God or man can eventually issue justice, then how much more will a God who loves us, who gave his only begotten son, who in turn suffered and endured the

cross, show us mercy? For the Bible says that he became obedient unto death, even the death of the cross, and that God has given him a name above every name and that at the name of Jesus every knee will bow, and every tongue shall confess that he is the Lord of Lords and the King of Kings.

> **RGWOE - What is the Point?** *No matter what type of resistance you encounter in life, you can either stop after the first knock on the door or you can keep knocking until the opportunity you are seeking opens the door and welcomes you in to reap the harvest that God has for you.*

RGWOE Lesson 10 - Keep Living and You Will Understand

Psalm 37:25 - I was young and now I am old, yet I have never seen the righteous forsaken or their children begging bread.

In preparing for the introduction of today's lesson, it occurred to me that I am going to need your assistance in helping me lay the framework for it. Follow me for just a little bit and I believe you will understand my approach. For those of us who grew up in the church or have spent some time in the church or around church people, there are some familiar phrases and certain words we hear and almost instinctively finish the rest of the statement. For example, if I say *he may not come when you want him*, you respond with, *but he is always on time*. If I state *weeping may endure for a night*, you reply with, *but joy comes in the morning*. When I say *God is good all the time* you reply with *all the time God is good*, and then lastly if I state *I once was young but now I am old, but I never seen the righteous forsaken*… But I need to pause here to determine if we really do understand what this means: *"I once was young but now I am old, yet I have not seen the righteous forsaken or his children begging for bread.* And so, I would like to hang a title on this lesson: *Keep Living and You Will Understand.*

If I could go back in history and change or correct a few things I have done in life, I would start with when I accepted my call to ministry. I would go back and tell all the parents to whom I tried to lecture on how to raise teenagers: I did not understand what you were going through but now that I have raised two

adult children. I understand. I would go back and say to all the people I tried to comfort after they lost a loved one, I truly did not understand but now that I have lost my momma, my sister, my father, and mother in-law, I understand your pain and your tears. Keep living and you will understand.

As we get older, we can only hope that we become wiser with age. Speaking of age, it is funny how life is when you have lived a little while and reflect back on things you heard or experienced as a child. You see, when I was child, I wanted to be older and now that I am older, sometimes I long to be younger. When you are young there are things that you just do not understand. When I was younger, Momma always told me to make sure I had clean underclothes on at all times. At the time I just did not understand what she meant by that but over the years and several visits to the emergency room, now I understand what Momma meant.

When I was a teenager, I would often hear the preacher say he who finds a wife finds a good thing and obtains favor from the Lord. At the time I did not understand what all that meant. I only knew that she looked good, and I wanted to make her my wife. But now that I am knocking on the door of thirty-eight years of marriage, I now understand the good thing and favor part. I often heard Momma say, "Lord, please let me live to see my children become adults. At the time I did not understand but now when I see my children and grandchildren, I understand what Momma meant. When that ole country preacher used to talk about an old, rugged cross, I did not understand, but one day Jesus entered my life and now I understand the power of the cross.

Let me tell you how I arrived at today's verses. There are so many other uplifting and encouraging texts from this 37th chapter of Psalm. For here is where you will find, "Fret not yourself because of evildoers; be not envious of wrongdoers!" You will find bold statements like, "Trust in the Lord and do good"; and lastly "Delight yourself in the Lord, and he will give you the desires of your heart." But these do not constitute the reason we join in learning the text today. No, today's lesson is about trying to understand how David arrived at such a point in his life in which he could boldly say, *I once was young but now I am old, yet I have not seen the righteous forsaken or his children begging for bread.*

Background - David was born in Bethlehem, the youngest son of Jesse of the tribe of Judah. David attained great popularity by killing the Philistine giant, Goliath, in combat. David, eventually the second king of the Israelites, was regarded as a model king and founded a permanent dynasty. He was not without his

failures and shortcomings. At one time David callously plotted the death in battle of one of his officers, Uriah the Hittite, so that he could marry Uriah's beautiful wife, Bathsheba. So, I believe as we look at this quick summary of David's highlights, you can see that he was a man that had lived through some tough things.

The First Question - How Old Was King David? - In reading this passage of scripture, a couple of questions need answering. The first for me, what was David's age at the time this was written? Research indicates that David died in 960 B.C. at the age of seventy. We know he was seventy years old because 1 Kings 2:11 says he reigned for 40 years, and 2 Samuel 5:4 says he began his reign at the age of thirty. So, while the scripture does not specifically give his age at the time he wrote these verses, we can conclude that he was between the age of forty and seventy. In other words, he had lived through some stuff which made him more than qualified to share that wisdom with us.

The Second Question – What was going on in David's Life? The second question that I pondered on involved what was happening in David's life to cause him to make such a declaration by which you and I are encouraged these thousands of years later. Let me suggest that David was living life, and in life we should take some time to reflect on how good God has been to us. I believe David was doing that, looking back over his life, and reflecting on just how good God had been to him over his life's journey.

Relevance in Today's World - So, we find ourselves in today's world. Maybe you are going through something, and you cannot understand how God would allow you to go through this crisis. To you I say, keep living and trusting in God and you will understand. You see, I did not understand the significance of Jesus taking the money out of the fish. But now I am older and have hit some financial lows and highs where there was no money in the checking account, and the credit cards were all maxed out, and the two good friends that I had did not have the resources to help me out. But God sent a check when I least expected it. He provided food and clothing for us when we did not think we would make it to the end of the month. So, now I understand Jesus supplying money from the unlikeliest of places: inside a fish.

When I was younger, I did not understand the story of the Centurion telling Jesus that his servant was sick unto death and that Jesus could just speak the word and his servant would be healed. But now that I am older, I can remember lying in that emergency room and the doctor could not figure out what was wrong

with me, and as I phased in and out of consciousness all I could hear was my pastor speaking a word: "Lord, heal this brother so he can go home and be with his family." So, I understand what the Centurion meant when he said, "Lord, just speak the word."

When I was younger, I did not understand why the preacher in that little country church would always get excited and loud when he talked about Jesus, but now that I am older, I understand why he was excited. Because when Jesus came into my life, he gave me a new walk and a new talk. I am excited because he said he would never leave me or forsake me. When I was a babe in Christ, I did not understand "let the words of my mouth and the meditations of my heart be acceptable in your sight." But now that I have lived a while I understand. For I just want to serve the Lord. I want to hear him say, "Well done, thou good and faithful servant." When I was younger and in my sin, I did not understand how God could love a wretch and sinner like me. I did not know why he cared for me when I did everything I could to avoid the church. But now that I am older, I understand he died that we could live. My friends, we may not understand every step that is before us, but know this, the Lord establishes our steps. So, the path may twist and turn and there may be some hills to climb, but when you get to the top you can look back and say, "I once was young and now I am older, and the Lord has been good to me."

> **RGWOE - What is the Point?** *Faith sometimes means you do not understand what God is doing in your life but trusting that He has your best interest at heart. Remember to ask God to give you peace until you gain an understanding.*

RGWOE Lesson 11 - Wait and Be of Good Courage

Isaiah 40:28–31 - Have you not known? Have you not heard? The Lord is the everlasting God, the Creator of the ends of the earth. He does not faint or grow weary; his understanding is unsearchable. He gives power to the faint, and to him who has no might he increases strength. Even youths shall faint and be weary, and young men shall fall exhausted; but they who wait for the Lord shall renew their strength; they shall mount up with wings like eagles; they shall run and not be weary; they shall walk and not faint.

My dear friends, over the years that I have been amongst church families, I have noticed that the congregations are blessed to have so many accomplished members. For someone who is just visiting they would not notice it because it is rarely if ever spoken of by you. For you serve humbly and graciously as a child of God. I have had the privilege and honor of being invited to your homes and your special celebrations and events, and I quickly realize that many if not all of you are movers and shakers. I surmise that in order to arrive at where you are in life, sitting around just waiting was not an option you employed. There are generals, sergeant majors, captains, doctors, lawyers, CEOs, petty officers, gunnery sergeants, master chiefs, admirals, principals, and administrators, just to name a few. I mean, you say a word and things start happening. You sign documents and activities take place, funds are transferred, people are hired, and office space is rented. While a mover and shaker attitude can drive us to success in life, it can sometimes cause us to struggle in life when it comes to us having to wait on God. It is with this as the backdrop that I would like to provide you with today's lesson: *Wait and Be of Good Courage.*

Allow me to first state that waiting is never easy, and let us face it, none of us like to wait. So, for the sake of understanding the context of today's lesson, come on and join me as I stop by the local grocery store in preparation for a snowstorm that may or may not happen. I only need five items, so it will not take me long to get there and get out of the place. I need milk, eggs, bread, toilet paper, and of course some coconut flavored Oreo cookies. So, I grab the few items from the shelves and head to the checkout counter. Since I do not want to wait, I see there is a short line at a terminal near the exit doors and I commit to jump in that line. But as I am standing behind the person ahead of me, this person cannot find their credit card, and after waiting for what seems like an eternity, they find the credit card but now their credit card will not work, and the line just stops. Since I do not like to wait, I look to my left and then to my right. I see a short line, so I bolt over there only to realize the cashier is in training and moving slow and then I see the dreaded "need assistance" light start flashing. Since I do not like waiting, I look over at the line I just left, and it is now starting to move. I could go on, but you know how the rest of the scenario will unfold. Waiting is never easy.

Retailers have capitalized on our inability to wait. You can bypass the long traffic line by using the express lanes. I went to Kings Dominion website to check out the prices of tickets and they have something called "Fast Lane Plus." It states, "Make the most of your day with a Fast Lane wristband that allows you to bypass the regular lines on some of your favorite attractions." I mean, who wants to wait to have fun? For the sake of transparency, I have yielded to the retailer's ploy. For lunch I like to go to my favorite restaurant also known as the greatest place on earth which is Chick-fil-A. But all too often I arrive at the restaurant, and the line is out the door, until one day I noticed a sign that said "avoid the line, download the app." So, I downloaded the app and when I walked in, I see all those people standing in line, but I skip the line, grab my meal, get in my car, and the smell of freshly cooked waffle fries places a smile on my face. But rest assured that I am not here to tell you that you are next in line for God's intervention because truth be known, I do not know who is ahead of you or who is behind you in line.

I need to provide you with some context of the scriptures. Isaiah is the first book in the section called Major Prophets. The prophet Isaiah wrote it at approximately 700 B.C. Isaiah contains some of the most incredible prophecies of any book. It contains foreknowledge, in incredible details about the Messiah, and the future reign of Jesus Christ. The purpose of the book of Isaiah was to call God's nation, the nation of Judah, back to faithfulness and to declare the coming Messiah. In Chapters 1-39, Isaiah points out the sins of both North and South Kingdoms. He then declares severe punishment to them and all the neighboring nations around them. In Chapters 40 - 55, he speaks of the return and restoration after the exile from Babylon.

First, Isaiah has to remind the people of who God is, for He says, "Have you not known, have you not heard?" I feel like the author is saying, "Let me school you and drop some knowledge on you; you'd better recognize who God is and what God can do." Second, *He does not faint or grow weary.* The text does not state how old Isaiah was at the time he authored this book, but I imagine he had experienced some things in life and looking back he says the youth and young men shall faint and become weary but they that wait on the Lord, their strength will be renewed. Oh, the young are just filled with boundless energy, but the author states that this group will not last. It is about how you wait on the Lord.

Wait on the Lord - Life at times can and will exhaust each one of us. There are some issues and challenges that we face that if we are not careful, we will try and fight it ourselves. And it seems the longer one waits for something to happen the more one thinks the outcome is not going to be in their favor. But let me remind you that to the weak He gives strength. "For they shall mount up with wings like eagles, they shall run and

not be weary." I love the fact that the author states *wings like an eagle*. So, if you see me standing still, if you should see me on bended knees and tears running down my face, do not feel bad or sad. Just know that I am waiting for my wings.

I want to be like the eagle, not the kiwi. The kiwi[9] is a flightless bird native to New Zealand. Kiwis cannot fly, have under-developed wing and chest muscles, and lack a sternum. This makes them particularly vulnerable to crushing injuries. Please, whatever you do, do not try and take off without your wings. Be like the eagle. An eagle will never surrender to its enemy, no matter its strength or size. It will always put up a fight to win or regain its territory. While other birds fly away from the storm, an eagle spreads its mighty wings and uses the current to soar to greater heights.

Relevance in Today's World. So, we are about to put last year into the history books forever and enter the new year. But last year did not deliver all the things you prayed for and wanted to happen for you and your family. I say wait and be of good courage. You have been working so hard to buy that home that you wanted but you have not closed the deal just yet. You have submitted hundreds of resumes and gone on numerous interviews but last year did not yield a job, or if it did it came with a significant decrease in salary and a longer commute. You have worked hard to increase your credit score, but it has not budged one inch. You have been waiting for the next promotion, but they gave it to someone else. Maybe you are single and desired a spouse, but last year brought you a curbside, garbage-material relationship. Or maybe last year you found out the wonderful marriage you thought you had is near its end and needs restoration. Wait and be of good courage. Please know that you are not alone; there are people who may be sitting by you right now and know that the struggle is real. But let me also remind you that we have some splendid examples of those who have experience in waiting on the Lord. There are some people who understand what it means to wait long and pray hard. When it was revealed to him that he would not die until the birth of Christ, Simeon waited for the birth of Christ. The woman with the issue of blood waited for twelve long years. The man who sat by the pool waited for thirty-eight years to receive this healing. So, waiting is nothing new; it has been around for a long time. The challenge is what you do while you are waiting.

Waiting with Expectations - Wait with great expectation, like a groom waiting for his bride to walk down the aisle. Like a first-time father waiting outside of the waiting room for the newborn baby to arrive. Like a mother who is at the front door waiting for her child to get off the school bus. Like parents waiting at the

---

[9] https://www.nationalgeographic.com/animals/article/rise-of-kiwi-bird-new-zealand November 10, 2021.

airport for their child who is serving in the military, now returning home from a tough duty assignment. These each wait with great expectation. Or like a father waiting in fear and trembling for the first-time teenage driver to pull into the driveway. Wait and be of good courage. If you cannot fly, then run, if you cannot run then walk, but let us not grow weary of doing good, for in due season we will reap if we do not give up. Waiting requires commitment, commitment requires perseverance, perseverance requires dedication and dedication requires waiting on the Lord.

In closing, allow me to share a story with you that at first annoyed me but turned out to be a moment of praise and revelation. A few years ago, an elementary school principal banned candy canes at her school due to what she said was its religious significance. The shape is a 'J' for Jesus. The red is for the blood of Christ, and the white is a symbol of his resurrection. Please know that as preachers we try to see the theological connection in just about everything we come across in life. But personally, up until the time of this story, I had never made that theological connection between Jesus and the candy cane. But now I have a moment of praise and revelation about the candy cane. You see, if the cane were big enough it could assist someone with walking. If the cane were strong enough, it could be used to help pull someone in need of help, and if it were put in my mouth, I would realize that the candy is sweet to the taste. So be of good courage knowing that is Jesus identified in the candy cane. You can lean on him in the walk of life. You can take courage in knowing that He can pull you out of whatever situation in which you find yourself. And while the candy cane is sweet, wait to know that we should taste and see that the Lord is good, and every day with Jesus is sweeter than the day before.

My dear friends, "be anxious for nothing, but in everything by prayer and supplication, with thanksgiving, let your requests be made known to God; and the peace of God, which surpasses all understanding, will guard your hearts and minds through Christ Jesus" (Philippians 4:6-7).

> **RGWOE - What is the Point?** *It is not about how long you wait but how you wait. So please do not blame others for delaying what you want or need, but trust that God will deliver on time and all the time.*

RGWOE Lesson 12 - Navigating Turbulence on the Way to Your Dreams

Genesis 37:10-11 - When he told his father as well as his brothers, his father rebuked him and said, "What is this dream you had? Will your mother and I and your brothers actually come and bow down to the ground before you?" His brothers were jealous of him, but his father kept the matter in mind.

Every year around the Christmas season, I look forward to watching television shows that remind me of what it is like to be a kid again. And one show that Brenda and I enjoy watching during the Christmas season is a movie about a little boy who wants a certain toy for Christmas. He has numerous dreams about how he will use this toy. As he puts it, it is the Holy Grail of Christmas gifts in an exclusive 1940s retro box, it is the Daisy Model 1938 Red Ryder BB gun with a 650-shot BB capacity[10]. It is the toy of Ralphie's dreams. Throughout the movie, Ralphie tells his teacher, his friends, the Santa at the mall, and his parents, and they all emphatically respond that he cannot get this gift because "you'll shoot your eye out." Ralphie experienced what I would like to refer to as *turbulence on the way to reaching his dream.*

Turbulence includes those moments of tough and unexpected encounters in life. This includes the rough moment, the unanticipated disturbance, and also the ordinary moment in time. For a point of reference, I am not an enthusiastic fan of flying. If I could drive everywhere I would do just that, drive. Just like when Brenda and I recently flew to Europe. If I could, I would have driven there, but there are two obstacles that prevent me from driving to Europe. First, there is not a bridge to cover the distance over the Atlantic, and second, Brenda would not ride shotgun with me. Nonetheless, flying serves its purpose. Once you are all settled in and on your way, you are just relaxing, reading magazines, playing games on your phone, or getting a long-needed nap. But all of sudden you will feel the aircraft hit what feels like bumps, and then that game or magazine you had in hand is replaced by some prayers and a quick swipe to find your Bible app. We have learned that those bumps are referred to as turbulence. Sometimes the pilot can predict when the turbulence will show up, but most times the turbulence comes unexpectedly and has no defined duration. And so, it is. I would like to leave you with the lesson: *Navigating the Turbulence on the Way to Your Dreams.*

To a certain degree most, if not all of us, can relate to the little boy in the movie dreaming of a toy that he really wants. It has been my experience that no matter how old or young you are, everyone has dreams. When I was younger, my number one dream job was to buy an 18-wheel tractor and trailer and drive across

---

[10] https://www.imdb.com/title/tt0085334/ November 10, 2021.

the country talking on my CB radio. That dream changed when I saw Brenda return from the military in uniform and the subsequent recruitment commercial. I dreamed about joining the military and becoming a mechanical engineer. I went to the recruiting station, took a few tests, and was informed that my test scores did not qualify me for mechanical engineering, but the recruiter said, "Don't you worry, have I got a deal for you! Since you want to do mechanical things, I'm going to send you to combat arms school to work with all kinds of heavy mechanical machinery." I never landed in that mechanical engineer position, so I have some personal experience with turbulence on the way to one's dreams.

Dreams stretch from where you currently are to where you desire to be. While I do not know your dreams, I am sure you have a few of them. In fact, I would dare say some of your dreams may have already come true. The challenging and most difficult part of life is how to navigate that turbulence until you reach the destination you seek. Sometimes we look at the people around us and they seem to have it all together. They are always smiling. You ask them how they are doing and hear phrases like "too blessed to be stressed" or "blessed and highly favored." It makes you wonder, am I living the right life because yesterday I hit some turbulence in my life and putting on the seat belt did not help; and I do not feel like I am too blessed to be stressed. In fact, I feel like I am too stressed to be blessed. Come on and be real with me. It takes time to navigate the difficult and unexpected challenges in life. But I believe that when we look at this story about Joseph, we can realize that while life can be difficult and has its twists and turns, God has a way of using those situations to take us to greater heights and greater service in doing the Lord's will.

The problem or challenge of living in such a demanding "right now" society is how to stay focused on the dreams for which you have worked so hard, and for which your parents have sacrificed so much. You have prayed about it and set forth in a direction to achieve the dreams. Dreams are ubiquitous in nature; it does not matter if you are young or old, black, white or brown, man or woman, everyone has dreams. Lord knows I have had my share of dreams and I hope that you have them as well.

So, our lesson begins with Joseph out in the field pasturing with his brothers. Joseph from the natural side had a few things going on that caused his brothers to target him for harm. He was young – only seventeen years old, and his father loved him more than the others and made him a robe of many colors. And if that was not enough, Joseph provided a performance appraisal on his brothers to his father, and it was not a good report. Of course, this resulted in his brothers hating him and never speaking peacefully to him. Then Joseph tells of a dream of how his sheave rises up and his brothers' sheaves worship him. I need to drop a quick footnote here. Be careful with whom you share your dreams. Not everyone is happy to hear them, not

everyone will try and support you, and some will even try and undermine them. In my mind, I can imagine his brothers thinking: wait a minute, you have given pops a bad report of our work ethic, pops has given you a luxurious coat that none of us have, and now you are here telling us we are going to bow down and worship you? Have you lost your mind? I mean, they already hated him, but this was a whole new level of dislike. In response to Joseph's dream, his brothers asked him two brief but insightful questions: "Are you indeed to reign over us? Or are you indeed to be preferred over us?"

As you navigate turbulence on the way to reaching your dreams, there are three things I want you to remember. First, be prepared for the haters. The word hate is used three times within this passage of text and the word dream is used at least ten times. From this perspective the dream numerically outnumbers the haters. So, do not be surprised that when you share your dreams with others, not everyone will be happy to hear your news. Joseph shared his dream with his brothers, and they hated him all the more. He shared his dream with his father and his father rebuked him. Your coworkers are happy with you until you tell them you have bigger dreams.

Can you imagine the intern calling a staff meeting with the CEO, COO, CFO, and everyone else with a title on the door and saying, "Last night I had a dream, and in my dream all of you reported to me? For starters, you, the CEO, are responsible for bringing me coffee." How do you think that meeting would have gone? For all of you in the military, you would likely look at it from this perspective: Imagine the private, fresh out of basic training, calling a command meeting and telling the generals, colonels, sergeant majors: "I had a dream and each one of you will report to me and must follow my orders."

Second, do not let setbacks hold you back. Joseph experienced some turbulence in his life. He was thrown in a cistern then sold into slavery. He ended up in a place where he was not known. He was hated by his brothers and rebuked by his father. He was sold for twenty pieces of silver and even spent time in prison. This is what I call significant turbulence.

Sometimes it takes longer than expected - Genesis 41:46 states that Joseph was thirty years old when he entered service for the pharaoh. When one reads the story of Joseph's dreams, and one hears what he went through, if we are not careful, we could conclude that, while the journey was filled with turbulence, it did not last exceptionally long. I submit to you that Joseph experienced some setbacks along the way. Allow me to put time into perspective for you. He was seventeen when he was sold into Egypt. At the age of thirty he became an overseer. He was thirty-nine when his brothers first came to Egypt and was probably forty-one or so when the brothers came a second time and Jacob moved to Egypt. While Joseph was obviously mistreated by his brothers and his father did not give him much encouragement when he expressed his dreams, he did not allow this mistreatment to become an excuse for him to treat them badly during their time of need. In fact, he did the exact opposite. He shared God's goodness with those who had intentionally meant to do him harm. The lesson here is that we should all do likewise. When you have successfully navigated the turbulence in pursuit of your dreams, remember to share that goodness with others. It took Joseph thirteen years to see and experience the blessing that he had envisioned when he was a teenager.

The challenge in life includes the navigation of the difficult spots on the way to your dreams. Do not allow the enemy to rob or steal your dreams, just because you experience some turbulence on the way to them. Have you ever daydreamed or had a dream about what you wanted to do or where to go in life? I am here to remind you that when we trust in God all things are possible. Joseph could have become discouraged or given up after all the things that happened to him along the way. He had endured much from his brothers, his father, and others who were in charge, but he decided to stay the course. Maybe you have given up on your dreams, or maybe life has thrown you for a bump and you do not see the dream before you. But Satan, life issues, and challenges can often cause interference on the way to your destination. Some may dislike you because of the dreams you are pursuing. Others may act against you. But nowhere in the text does it indicate Joseph gave up on his dreams. Some wanted to kill him because of his dream but he stayed the course. What will you do the next time you experience some turbulence in life? May I suggest we take note of what the airline does. Let the pilot guide you through, and the pilot is Jesus Christ.

> **RGWOE - What is the Point?** *When you hit the rough spots, sometimes you have to buckle up and hold on tight, knowing that Jesus is the pilot of your life, and no co-pilot is needed or required.*

RGWOE Lesson 13 - Sometimes It Is Not the Mountain That Needs to Move

Deuteronomy 1:6-7 *The L*ORD *our G*OD *said to us at H*OREB, *"Y*OU *have stayed long enough at this* MOUNTAIN. *Break camp and advance into the hill country of the Amorites; go to all the neighboring peoples in the Arabah, in the mountains, in the western foothills, in the Negev and along the coast, to the land of the Canaanites and to Lebanon, as far as the great river, the Euphrates.*

I would like to call your attention to the sixth verse where it states, "The Lord our God said to us in Horeb, 'You have stayed long enough at this mountain.'" Many years ago, when Brenda and I were stationed in Germany, the church we attended identified a married couple in need of a place to stay and wanted to know if we would welcome them into our home for a few days, and of course, we did welcome them to our home. They were a nice couple, and we enjoyed the pleasure of their conversation after work. A few days went by, and they had made themselves comfortable by buying their own groceries. Then days turned into weeks and weeks turned into months, and then to top things off, I started noticing different things like items in my pantry were being swapped out for things I just do not like. What I realized at that time is that this couple had become completely comfortable about making decisions in a home that they did not live in. In other words, they had stayed long enough in the Gaines' household. And so, I would like to leave with you the lesson: *Sometimes It Is Not the Mountain That Needs to Move.*

The use of the word mountain is prevalent throughout church culture. There is an abundance of songs that speak about mountains. We are familiar with songs like "Go Tell It on the Mountain"[11] and "Lord, Do Not Move the Mountain" by Mahalia Jackson[12]. In American culture, we sing about the mountains with *O beautiful for spacious skies, for amber waves of grain, for purple mountain majesties…*[13] Okay, let me come a little closer to where you live; we reminisce of bygone days with lyrics like: *ain't no mountain high enough to keep me from getting to yo*u[14]. Which begs the question, why are mountains such a well-known descriptor in our lives?

My friend, I believe mountains can be seen as obstacles, but in the same breath we are often awed by the beauty and splendor of rock formations that God has created on this earth. Then from a military geographical perspective, mountains can be viewed as a point of advantage or disadvantage depending on where one is

---

[11] https://hymnary.org/text/while_shepherds_kept_their_watching November 10, 2021.
[12] https://genius.com/Mahalia-jackson-lord-dont-move-the-mountain-lyrics November 10, 2021.
[13] https://hymnary.org/text/o_beautiful_for_spacious_skies November 10, 2021.
[14] https://genius.com/Marvin-gaye-and-tammi-terrell-aint-no-mountain-high-enough-lyrics November 10, 2021.

standing. Nonetheless, mountains can provide protection and comfort that may cause one to not want to leave. It is always easy to want the mountains to move. But not every mountain in our lives is the problem. Sometimes the problem is ourselves. Boom! There it is. I know it is a shocker but follow me for a few minutes.

Today we find ourselves reading texts from the Old Testament in the book of Deuteronomy. Yes, Deuteronomy, I know it is a word that is probably only heard during a sermon or Bible study class. Ponder this for a moment, when was the last time you saw a bumper sticker or hashtag that contained the word Deuteronomy? As believers we quote our favorite scriptures all the time, and I personally have no recollection of anyone ever telling me that their favorite scripture from the Bible came from the book of Deuteronomy. Since awareness of the book is limited or unknown, allow me a few moments to tell you about the book of Deuteronomy.

The book of Deuteronomy is the fifth book in the Old Testament. It is the last book that Moses wrote, ending at his death and the eventual rise of his assistant, Joshua, and his leadership over the nation of Israel. In Ancient Greek, it is "Deuteronómion" which means "second law" or a "copy of the law," signifying a re-telling of God's laws. In essence it is a retelling, a repetition, or a reminder of the covenant that God made with His people. If there was a movie made after this book it would be called the *Ten Commandments: The Remake* starring Charlton Heston or Harrison Ford.

The place where they were encamped was in the plain, in the land of Moab, where they were just ready to enter Canaan and engage in a war with the Canaanites. Yet Moses discourses not to them concerning military affairs, the arts, and stratagems of war, but concerning their duty to God. In a series of farewell messages, Moses exhorts the new generation of Israelites to live as his obedient people in the promised land. As his final act at this momentous time of transferring leadership to Joshua, Moses delivered his farewell address to prepare the people for their entrance into Canaan. This leads us to the sixth verse where it states, "You have stayed long enough." May I park here for a few minutes? The question on the floor is what mountains have you been on for too long? While we are not at Mount Horeb, there are situations, places, and people about which God has said: you have been around for too long; it is time for you to move. We pray, and we pray that God will move the jerk of a boss that you have been dealing with, but my dear friend, maybe it is not the boss that needs to move. Maybe you find yourself dealing with toxic and unhealthy friendships and you want to move but just do not know how. Do not get too comfortable. Maybe it is time for you to move on.

The Israelites had walked for forty years, so I can imagine that they had gotten comfortable in their current state. I do not know about you, but I like being comfortable. While the text does not specifically say they had gotten comfortable, I can imagine that they were just like most of us in that they had gotten into a routine. They had been at this for a while, and you and I know that the longer you do something the more comfortable and less likely you are to want to change. God had to serve them an eviction notice. For my military folks, God informed them that they had been on station too long and he was issuing them a set of PCS orders.

Three key points to remember from today's lesson:

Turn and take your journey - Moses is telling the people to turn and take your journey. Do not miss this point. He does not say take a trip because they would have just focused on getting from point A to point B. Know this: it is about the journey when it is not the mountains that need to move. The Christian walk is about the journey.

Let me tell you a few things about this journey. It can and will be fraught with challenges, difficulties, twists, and turns. This journey will take you to hilltop experiences followed by some valley lows. This journey has promotions and demotions. It has moments of laughter intertwined with bittersweet tears. On this journey one will often encounter roadblocks and detours. This journey will sometimes make you ask the question: Lord, why me? But nonetheless we must turn and take the journey. The Israelites had to wander in the wilderness for forty years for their lack of faith and confidence in what God would give them in the promised land. How many of us miss out on the promises of God because the journey is fraught with what we perceive as giant obstacles? We fail to remember that the God we serve can do exceedingly abundantly above all that we ask or think, according to the power that works in us.

God was giving them instructions to go right back to the place where they just went, through fighting and winning over their enemy, and now He was essentially telling them: you have stayed too long. My momma used to tell me, "Make people happy twice—once when you show up and the second time when you leave their presence." In other words, do not overstay your welcome. But it is hard. When you have been in one place for so long you get comfortable. Lest I be a hypocrite, I want you to know I love being comfortable. Man, once I am comfortable it is hard for me to move because I am comfortable in my mountain location. I know where everything is; I know the people. I know the short cuts. I know the weather patterns. And besides, we have been wandering forty years and most people that once were with us are no longer. I love this mountain spot location.

Go and take possession - Allow me to make a point of clarification on the taking of possession. Notice Moses makes it clear to take possession of what God swore to them. He did not say take possession of whatever you want but only what God had promised. So, there is no need for any of us to feel that God has left us out when we see those around us being blessed in mighty and magnificent ways. For the same God who placed it on our neighbors or friends never runs out of the goodness that he wants to bestow upon us. While in this story the author is referring to the territories, in today's world the same theology applies to every aspect of our lives. There is an old song that says: *I am taking back everything that the devil has stolen from me.*[15] What is keeping you from taking the next step in your life?

I am reminded of the story of King David. One day King David came home to a city called Ziklag. But while he was gone, the enemy came into Ziklag and stole everything David had. But you see, David encouraged himself in the Lord, and he made up his mind. He said, "I am on my way down to his cave and I am taking back what is rightfully mine." So, while on this journey you have to encourage yourself in the Lord. I am taking back what the devil has had influence over in my life. I am taking back my song, my dance, my joy, and my peace. Can I get an Amen?

Take the Lord along with you. - While I have already given two key points, these points do not mean much if you do not have the third point. My last point is simply this: take the Lord along with you. So, while you are moving away from the mountain, and you have made that turn to start the journey, do not forget to take the Lord along with you. It does not matter where we go in life, we are going to need the Lord on our side. So, fight a good fight, keep the faith, and never give up.

> **RGWOE - What is the Point?** *Do not let your comfort zone become the obstacle that blocks you from seeing what is on the other side of the mountain. So, dig deep, find the steepest part of the mountain, and start climbing one step at a time, and do not stop until you have reached the other side of the mountain.*

---

[15] https://genius.com/Dorinda-clark-cole-take-it-back-lyrics November 10, 2021.

RGWOE Lesson 14 - A Hard Test and a Good Report Card

2 Chronicles 9:1-2 - Now when the queen of Sheba heard of the fame of Solomon, she came to Jerusalem to test Solomon with hard questions, having a very great retinue, camels that bore spices, gold in abundance, and precious stones; and when she came to Solomon, she spoke with him about all that was in her heart. So Solomon answered all her questions; there was nothing so difficult for Solomon that he could not explain it to her.

Let us talk about report cards for a second. Report cards reflect one's actions and behavior during their classes at school or college. So please try and liken this correlation to King Solomon's because the text indicates that the Queen of Sheba had heard a report of King Solomon's actions and behavior. So, she asked King Solomon some challenging questions because she wanted to test his knowledge and validate the report she had heard about him. It should be noted that no one likes tough questions. I really was not aware of how I handled hard questions until a few years back at my birthday party. My so-called friends (lol) decided to roast me a little bit, and to my surprise they informed me that when I encounter hard questions, I make certain noises and sounds, because the hard questions made me feel uncomfortable. And so it is today that we find ourselves in the midst of an intriguing story between a queen and a king with the lesson: *A Hard Test and a Good Report Card.*

Let us admit it right from the start that most, if not all of us, dislike tests. And you have heard my personal struggle in the land of academia about the results of tests in the early years of my life. Do you remember the time before there were smartphones and websites? Before technology arrived, the schools would actually send the report card home with the student to hand to Momma. Believe me when I say there were a lot of report cards that did not make that journey home. With that being said, if you were to go back to the elementary school I attended and take a jack hammer and break up the street that separated the school bus from the school entrance, you will find report cards buried there. I will not confirm or deny that the report cards you find buried under said street may or may not belong to Jeffery E. Gaines of the third, fourth, and fifth grade. But before I proceed, the tradition of any preacher allows me a few minutes to set the context of today's lesson. Today we find ourselves reading from the Old Testament book of 2nd Chronicles. The book is interesting in that 2nd Chronicles covers the time from Solomon's ascension to the throne (971 BC) until the southern kingdom of Judah was finally carried into exile in Babylon in 586 BC. The chronicler portrayed Jewish history, focusing on the blessings God bestowed when leaders were faithful to His Law.

Who is the Queen of Sheba? - Our lesson starts off with the entrance of the Queen of Sheba. My research indicates Sheba was a kingdom in African Ethiopia. In its prime, Sheba was known as a wealthy kingdom which grew rich through trade along the incense routes between southern Arabia and the port of Gaza on the Mediterranean Sea. In today's world, the Queen of Sheba's arrival would not have made the mainstream media; there would have been no paparazzi snapping pictures and no celebrities posing for a group selfie. I make this assertion because it may surprise you to know that there is still a Queen of Sheba. Imperial Majesty, the Nubia-Sheba,[16] Empress of the African Royal Kingdoms, the Queen of Sheba, Queen Sheba III. This queen had all the wealth and riches of her kingdom at her disposal, for the Bible states she arrived with a retinue and spices. A retinue is a body of persons "retained" in the service of a noble, royal personage, dignitary, or "retainers."

Testing of the king - The text clearly states that when she heard of Solomon's fame, she came to Jerusalem to test him with hard questions. I have never been a good test taker. In fact, while in college I deferred all of my hard classes until the very last semesters of my program. I would advise anyone not to do that; it just meant that I had the most difficult classwork all at once and back-to-back. I know I am not alone when I say most of us have gone through some type of testing. While the queen's test was based on questions, in today's world our tests are often found in the issues or challenges of life. It could be the person sitting in the cubicle next to you that can test your last nerve. A simple engagement with the wait staff at a restaurant can test your patience just after you've dined on a fine meal. But life's hardest tests go beyond the mundane events of life. True hard tests are those tests that rock your world. A hard test is one that will keep you up all night praying and looking for an answer to the challenging questions of life. True tests are sometimes filled with disappointments and let downs.

What type of questions did the queen ask? - The Bible does not indicate the amount and types of questions she asked, but we can imagine that her responses in verses 3 and 4 provide some insight into the possibility of her inquiries. She states that after she experienced the house, the food of his table, the seating of his officials, and the attendance of his servants and their clothing, his cupbearers, and their clothing, and the burnt offerings that he offered at the house of the Lord, there was no more breath in her.

---

[16] https://www.african-royal-kingdoms.com/shebah-iii-queen-of-sheba-nubian-na November 10, 2021.

Solomon's Report Card - The queen tells Solomon that the report was true. Someone somewhere had created a report card on Solomon's behavior and his actions. For those of you who have long since forgotten about report cards, let me remind you of what they are. A report card communicates a student's performance academically. A typical report card uses a grading scale to determine the quality of a student's schoolwork. Traditional school report cards contained a section for teachers to record individual comments about the student's work and behavior. Hear me now: the people that were telling the queen about Solomon were in fact giving her a report card on Solomon's work and behavior. By all accounts from the Bible, the queen had heard the report but did not necessarily believe it, so she decided to go and administer an in-person verbal questionnaire to Solomon to determine if the report card was accurate. Ah, can you see the point I am slipping in? Our actions speak volumes about who we are and what we do. Is not that like the Super Bowl of testimonies when someone hears about how you are living your life and wants to come and see for themselves how the Lord is moving in your life.

After you have gone through the tests of life, what will your report card look like to those with whom you have come in contact over your journey? Let us strive to live a life that reflects love and concern for those we have met, those we know well, and even those we contact in some indirect way. Let us live a life that will literally take someone's breath away when they see how good God has been to us. They have seen your report card and want to see if the lifestyle matches up with the report. If you were receiving a report card today, what kind of grade would you receive? Please know that when we are being tested, we are not alone because others have gone before us and passed their tests, so likewise we can pass our tests in life. For instance, Paul was tested when he was shipwrecked, beaten, faced robbers, and was placed in jail. So, my friend, after you have gone through the tests of life, what will your report card look like to those with whom you have come in contact throughout your journey?

> **RGWOE - What is the Point?** *There are tests in life and there are no short cuts to the answers. Sometimes we have to answer the tough questions to the best of our ability, and that is all God requires us to do, which is our absolute best to serve him.*

RGWOE Lesson 15 - Undefeatable Determination

2 Corinthians 4:8-9 *- We are pressed on every side by troubles, but we are not crushed. We are perplexed, but not driven to despair. We are hunted down, but never abandoned by God. We get knocked down, but we are not destroyed.*

Today we find ourselves reading from 2nd Corinthians the 4th chapter around about the eighth verse. For background purposes, 2nd Corinthians is a book that Paul the Apostle wrote to the church to try to encourage its members. Within this book we will find some immensely powerful passages that will encourage us along life's journey. This book reminds us of just how challenging and difficult life can be when we want to live a life according to the Bible and a life that is reflective of Jesus Christ himself. So, I do not mean to bore you today, but I know that in this world all of us are determined to do something. Some of us are determined to do the right thing and then there are others who are determined to do the wrong thing. Accordingly, I want to speak to those who are trying to do the right thing, the right way according to God's Word and not according to what humans say; not according to what the favorite quote of the day is, and not according to the bumper sticker on the car that just drove by, but according to the gospel of Jesus Christ.

Therefore, for a few moments I would like to write about undefeatable determination. We live in a world where challenges seem to rise up at every turn, every crossroad, in multiple emails, twisted with Twitter and then basically on every Facebook post. How can we overcome the temptation of feeling defeated? I often look at athletes as an inspiration to achieve remarkable things. For example, I am fascinated that in the boxing world, Mr. Floyd Mayweather Jr. boxed from 1996 through 2015. During that period, he held multiple titles and retired with an undefeated record. I am sure I do not have to remind each of you that Mr. Mayweather did not do this in a haphazard way. He did not take an easy path nor did any of his opponents just roll over in the ring and say, "Punch me, knock me out, and go get your championship belt." No, Mr. Mayweather had to have great determination and perseverance.

When we look in the scriptures, we see that they talk about being perplexed, but not driven to despair. "We are hunted down, but never abandoned by God. We get knocked down, but we are not destroyed." My friend, the problem with trouble is that it shows up uninvited, it stays too long, and does not care about your situation or your circumstance. Needless to say, we are in the midst of some troubling times: racism is running rampant across the country, COVID-19 is causing increased fatalities each day, unemployment is at a record level, and our children are faced with the complexities of remote learning for the foreseeable future. How can

someone who is in the midst of all this chaos stay focused or encouraged during such troubling times? I am so glad you asked this question. I believe the answer lies within the Bible's numerous passages that address the topic of troubles. Verses like Nehemiah 8:10: "Do not grieve, for the joy of the Lord is your strength," and Psalm 46:1-3: "God is our refuge and strength, an ever-present help in trouble." Hence, no matter what trouble you find yourself dealing with; maybe it is the separation from family and friends; maybe you are facing divorce or a separation that you do not want; maybe it is the fear of not finding a respectable job to make ends meet. Let me remind you that God is our very present help in the time of trouble. So, no matter how dark the day or how bumpy life gets, God is still on the throne. Consequently, my words of encouragement for you today are, do not let your troubling situation steal your joy, especially when your joy is in the Lord and all that He has done for you, for one day, this too shall pass. No matter where you are or where you have been, God is with you. Consequently, my friend, while we are in the midst of troubling times, God is still in control. Therefore, today I want you to stand up, pray up, read up, and move up to where God wants you to be. We must refuse to allow trouble to derail the future that God has for us.

We are perplexed, but not driven to despair. Life can be baffling at times by what people say and do to each other. Sometimes you just want to throw your hands up and walk away. Let me remind you, we are not in despair, for God is living on the street you call home and is in the seat next to you on the train as you commute to work. He is in the third grade classroom and deploys soldiers who serve in a hot spot in a foreign land. So do not despair. Hang on to your undefeatable determination regarding thinking and doing. That is why we never give up. Paul encourages us to never give up. All too often there is a tendency in our culture to flee in the face of challenges that seem impossible to overcome. Let me confirm what you probably already know: if you give up, there is a 100% guarantee that you will not reach your stated goals. However, if you never give up, there is a higher probability that you will not only achieve your goals, but in many cases, God will take you beyond your initial plans. Just know that it takes undefeatable determination to get there.

I want you to know that in our Christian walk, we have to always remain undefeated in our determination. In today's world, people are determined to do a lot of things, and some of them are remarkable things, but some of them are not so smart. Sometimes people are determined to put themselves in harm's way just to go viral. Sometimes people are determined to do something so ridiculous that they overlook the dangers and tragedies that are consequences to their actions. I want to remind each of you that the devil came and tried to defeat grace; but aren't you glad that we serve an undefeatable God? The Bible says that they whipped Jesus and put him on a cross, drove spikes into his hands and spikes into his feet. The Romans tried to defeat Him for they sent him from judgment hall to judgement hall. The Bible says that they put him in a tomb

and that they sealed it with a large stone, and not only did they seal it with a stone, they placed guards at the entrance because they wanted to defeat the purpose of Christ's mission here on this earth. But the Bible says that on the third day he rose from the grave, and when he rose from the grave all those forces that were determined to keep Him in the grave could no longer do so, for he rose up with all power. They pierced his side, thinking that would for sure finally stop his heart from beating forever, but He did come down from that cross and he did rise from the grave.

I submit to you today that in this life people and things are determined to get in our way. Will you have an undefeatable determination? "For I am persuaded that nothing will separate us from the love of God: not height, nor depth, not angels or demons. Indeed, nothing shall separate us from the love of God" (Romans 8:38-39). You have to be determined today; you have to press on even when you do not feel like it. You have to look beyond your circumstances; you have to be determined to say I am just going to hold on and see what God is going to do. I am determined to live a life that would be pleasing to God. I am determined to be the best single I can be. I am determined to be the best spouse I can be because I have undefeatable determination.

> **RGWOE - What is the Point?** *How determined are you in life? Will you allow a problem to derail who you are? Will you use your faith to derail the problem?*

RGWOE Lesson 16 - A Day Like No Other Day – We All Have Them

Joshua 10:12-13 *On the day the L*ORD *gave the Amorites over to Israel, Joshua said to the L*ORD *in the presence of Israel: "Sun, stand still over Gibeon, and you, moon, over the Valley of Aijalon." So, the sun stood still, and the moon stopped, till the nation avenged itself on its enemies, as it is written in the Book of Jashar. The sun stopped in the middle of the sky and delayed going down about a full day.*

I am reminded of a TV commercial about insurance. In this commercial it shows the lives of two individuals, and as they are showing the two characters, they are saying the same words and phrases: "I cannot believe this is happening to me." However, they are both having two extremely distinct kinds of day. On one side of the equation, there is this young lady, and it appears that her father is buying her a first car. On the other side of the equation there appears to be the business executive returning to his car, but it has been ravaged by vandals. And they both say the same phrase: "I cannot believe this happening to me, what a day," because they were having a day like no other. Hence it is that I would like to direct your attention to the Joshua 10:14, for it states there has been no day like it before or since. In reading this passage, it is important to understand how we arrived at this moment in time. I need to a take few moments to provide you with the context of this lesson. I am sure the question is asked: why do preachers always talk about context? What you may not realize is that at some point in time each of you were probably a contextual speaker. Follow me for a few minutes. Do you remember as a child or as a teenager you had gotten into trouble, and you knew Momma was going to tighten you up as soon as she arrived home? But just as Mom was about to tighten you up, you said, "Momma, please let me explain," because you were thinking if you could provide her with the context of what was happening before she saw you doing something stupid, it would change or influence her decision. This is why preachers provide biblical context, we are hoping to influence your thinking about Bible verses that were written a long time ago.

Most of us are familiar with Joshua's triumphant victory at the city of Jericho when the walls came down. But what is often overlooked is that Joshua went up to the city of Ai and received his butt whipping. However, the second time around, Joshua sustained a victory against the City of Ai. So, this is where we find ourselves here in Joshua the tenth chapter. While I did not cover the first seven verses, please allow me to do an executive summary on the events that were occurring.

The king of Jerusalem heard how Joshua had captured the cities of Jericho and Ai and devoted them to destruction. He also heard that the city of Gibeon had partnered with Joshua. The king knew that Gibeon was a great and noble city; it was full of warriors, and if Joshua had victory over Ai and a partnership with this powerful city, they did not stand a chance in battle against Joshua. As a result, the king decided to call other kings from the region and informed them of the situation. After hearing the situation, they all agreed to fight together and decided that they would go and attack Gibeon. Let me pause here for a moment. Can you see how this is going down? They knew he did not stand a chance against Joshua, so rather than attack Joshua they figured they would attack someone who had become close to Joshua. You know how it goes; Satan does not always come at us straight on but goes after someone that is close to us. For in Satan's way of thinking, he cannot affect you, so instead of going after the wife, he will go after the husband. Instead of attacking the parents he goes for the children; if he cannot get to the pastor he goes after the members. Can I get an amen?

That being said, we find ourselves back to the 8th verse, and there we see God telling Joshua, "Fear not for I have delivered them into your hands." I can imagine Joshua was not oblivious to these massive armies moving toward the city of Gibeon. But God comforted his heart and said fear not. Interesting point, when Joshua heard this, he marched quickly. When God tells us something, there is no time to call a study group or send out a survey. We have to move and move out quickly.

The next passage of scripture states that God threw the enemy into a state of panic. He tells the sun and the moon to stop in their place of orbit. Really? When we read this, it is easy to say, "Wow! Look at God," and that would be a correct response. But I would like to add that this is the same God that made heaven and earth, the same God that parted the Red Sea, so in my mind, stopping the sun and the moon would not be a problem—just saying.

We all have what I would like to coin as a day like no other. I could walk through a potential day that I would consider such a day. Please note that a day like no other day is not always relegated to just the challenges of life. For when Peter was walking on the water and began to sink and Jesus pulled him up from the water, Peter was having a day like no other day. When the woman with the issue of blood touched the hem of his garment, she was having a day like no other day, and conversely when the blind man was given his sight, he was having a day like no other. Let me remind you that Job had a day like no other, the three Hebrew boys had a day like no other. I imagine when Moses was fleeing from Egypt and pharaoh's army was in high

pursuit, Moses could have said, "This is a day like no other." When Paul was shipwrecked and bitten by a serpent, it was a day like no other. Well, that is fine and good, but how is this relevant to us today? Allow me to give some examples of what you and I would consider a day like no other.

If tomorrow morning you received a call at 9:35am from the mortgage company, and they say, "Do not send another payment because it is paid in full," it would be a day like no other. If the credit union called you and said, "We know you have made three payments on your brand-new car, but it is paid in full," it would be a day like no other. But wait, if the student loan officer called you and said, "Your student loans are paid in full, and to show you love, we are refunding every payment you have already made," that would be a day like no other. While these hypothetical situations are good, they do not compare to the day the Son stood still. And I am not talking about the sun; I am referring to the Son who is the Christ, the Son of God. For Christ stood before the court and he never said a mumbling word. He died and rose up, and that was a day like no other day. Christ paid a debt He did not owe. When I decided to give my life to Christ, that was a day like no other day.

> **RGWOE - What is the Point?** *I do not know what kind of day you are having, but I do know a savior that can change every day of your life. Do not get me wrong. You will still have daily battles, but the difference is you will have Christ to help you fight every battle, and you will say, "I just had a day like no other day."*

About the Author

Reverend G's educational achievements include a master's degree in practical theology from Regent University and a master's degree in public administration from Troy State University. Jeff has earned numerous awards to include the Army Superior Unit Award, the Civilian Meritorious Service Medal, five Army Achievement Medals, four Army Commendation Medals, four Army Good Conduct Medals, National Defense Service Medal, Superior Civilian Service Award, and two Meritorious Service Medals.

Reverend G is married to his childhood sweetheart, Brenda. They live in Lakewood Ranch, Florida, and have two podcast programs with international audiences.

- https://anchor.fm/RGWOE
- https://rg-woe.com/

Printed in the United States
by Baker & Taylor Publisher Services